STRIPED BASS ROMANCE

THE 60 +++ LB CLUB

TONY CHECKO

authorHOUSE®

AuthorHouse™
1663 Liberty Drive
Bloomington, IN 47403
www.authorhouse.com
Phone: 833-262-8899

Published by AuthorHouse 04/08/2022

ISBN: 978-1-6655-1434-7 (sc)
ISBN: 978-1-6655-1440-8 (e)

Print information available on the last page.

Any people depicted in stock imagery provided by Getty Images are models, and such images are being used for illustrative purposes only.
Certain stock imagery © Getty Images.

This book is printed on acid-free paper.

CONTENTS

CONTENTS

SUMMARY

Thirty years ago I saw her surf fishing. A woman surf casting was a rare sight at any time of the year. We had a brief conversation, luncheon and hoped to meet again. Being a fishing columnist and a spot at the local radio station, I gave her a few tips where bigger bass may be found. Her government job tended to keep her on the move, but she did find time to catch a 60 pound bass in one of the hotspots I mentioned. Weeks later we celebrated near the same spot where we first met. The celebration lead to more than dinner and dancing. I, TC, never saw her again.

Thirty years later TC lost his wife and moved to their seashore cottage. The only known relative, Ted, contacted him at the loss of his wife. Ted's wife was a relative of TC and had to leave for Europe on a month's business trip. Ted figured he would spend some time with TC and console the loss of his wife and pick up surf fishing passion lost while in college. TC reviewed with Ted the elements of surf fishing based on TC's years of talking and writing about it from rods, reels, bait and lures. TC talked to Ted about the basics. After lunch they strolled the beach talking about how to read the water.

After dinner TC got a phone call and had to leave immediately. He told Ted to catch up on surf fishing by reading the book in his library. Ted takes plenty of notes from the old and new writers as Lyman, Wollner, Daignault, Karas and others. TC returns to get some photos and starts to tell Ted about the events of 30 years ago. He said he will complete the story later as he must leave now. Ted returns to taking notes on other books in the library.

When TC returns he tells Ted the balance of the story. The phone call was from the daughter of the woman, Katie, he met surf fishing 30 years ago. The daughter's name is Kate, his daughter. Wow … TC never knew. Thirty years ago, Katie, left for the West Coast. Kate was born quietly hence kept TC marriage intact. TC and his wife never had children. Now TC found out he has a child. Katie died in Los Angeles due to an automobile accident. She told her daughter all about the East Coast fisherman at that time. Katy came back to the East to meet with TC. She was also in the same business as her mother and also part of the conservation program for striped bass in California. Her visit with her Dad was combined with the trip to Maryland where the East Coast striped bass tagging program was run. She sent a copy of the tagging program to TC if he promised to go to Los Angeles to meet his grandkids, a boy and a girl. TC says yes. She had to fly back to Los Angeles to combat the efforts to dump toxic chemicals in the waterways that habit by striped bass. TC and Ted review the tagging program.

TC calls Greg Myerson to congratulate him on catching his world record striped bass. Greg heard of TC through his radio and fishing column. Greg sends him the story of his 3-60 pound striped bass caught in one season as well as his world record 81.88 pound bass. TC and Ted review the stories.

TC and Ted continued their vacation surf fishing for the rest of the month. They got their fill of bass fishing. TC got ready to leave for California and Ted looked to his wife returning from her European trip.

PREFACE

This is not a novel about fictional events. This is a novel about striped bass and fishing. Most of the book contains facts with confirmed or subjective data gathered by the best fishermen since books have been written about fishing. It's a teaching novel but not a book like show and tell. Questions and answers are presented in a conversational atmosphere between two fishermen.

Fictitious names have been added to add cohesion to the story. Chapters are interwoven like a novel but could stand alone as separate subjects. Romance is the glue that cements the love of fishing with the unexpected love between a man and a woman.

Review of old and new fishing books you may have not read. Authors tell what you should know. Their secrets are laid out before you to keep and use. These authors are or were the best of the best writers. Their accomplishments are highlighted in numerous periodicals and their record fish are in the respected fishing journals worldwide. So here you have a novel concerning the ABC and the XYZ of surf fishing.

The chapter on tagging striped bass and the story of the world record bass are all based on facts. Greg Myerson's story about catching three striped bass over 60 pounds in one season is true and a very rare event. The story of his world record striped bass of 81.88 pounds was taken face- to face by the author.

The Striped Bass 60++ Club list has been updated with

additional members; it is now the Striped Bass 60+++ Club. If I missed you, let me know.

Latest regulations for commercial and recreational striped bass fishing by State.

STRIPED BASS ROMANCE

ACKNOWLEDGMENTS

Dr. Staut Welch

If all the railroads started at Washington DC terminal which one would you take to learn about the striped bass tagging program. Don't ask me ask Dr. Welch. He put me on the right railroad track which eventually led me to one website containing nearly over 700 pages of technical data. This was the right railroad track thank God I was on the right one and not on the wrong one.

Beth Versak

I am at the right terminal and Beth was the conductor. She guided me to other members of the staff and refined the parts of the striped bass tagging program which might interest me. She was very cordial and happy to talk to a lost passenger on this railroad track. She was key of getting information about the tagging program in Maryland, the focus hub of the program.

Sherwood Lincoln

An author himself, book about commercial fishing for striped bass, suggested various means to improve the novel as well as incorporate the basic understanding of surf fishing for striped bass. Since there hasn't been a book written like a novel for striped bass fishing, his comments were instructive and his suggestions important. There is my book review of Sherwood's book about the life of a 'pin' fisherman. If you are looking for tricks of the trade, Sherwood has the answers.

Kathy Malfi

I gave Kathy bits and pieces of my book before much of it was done. This was unfair but with her background as a book critic she plowed through it and did an enormous amount of work while I struggled with the rest of the book. Many of her suggestions enormously improved the conversation between the principal parties in the book she read it as a non-angler but as an interested person reading a new novel. A difficult task.

Al Ristori

Noted author, fishing editor of a New Jersey newspaper, captain of his boat, charters during the season, and a member of the 60+++ pound club, a friend and advisor.

Al was an editor of the early texts full of my errors and mixing up of some of the 46 saved scripts and sending it to him. A patient man he must be. If the ocean gets tough with the boat, he's the man you want at the helm. Fishermen must be patient. Successful ones are humble by their catch and hopeful in the future.

Al is successful at the helm and at the computer. Thanks Al.

Fran Glica

Fran could be considered a co-author. Not familiar with fishing lingo, she focused on the English. If she understood it, fishermen and women would have the same success.

Writing and rewriting make everything better and with a keen eye and a dictionary imbedded in her mind, she hunted and found the obvious and hidden poorly written text.

Where anglers might overlook errors of English, Fran was the 'English' angler with rod and reef in hand. Dot the i's and cross the t's, was her forte. Readability is the foundation of any story as rod and reel is the necessary tools of the fishermen. Thanks Fran, without you this book would be in rough waters.

Wife, kids, friends and interested parties, said 'go for it.' I did with help of the Dragon naturally speaking computer program. It helped get something down in the monitor and to the paper.

Perfect it isn1t but it saved hours of typing. It also offers time to make changes as it misunderstand your words. The more you use it the smatter it gets.

Diane Christofortti

Mr. S. Homes has nothing over Diane. The 'its and bits' that was missing she found. Super detective found what could not be found by other third party readers. Fresh eyes and a dictionary laden mind eased the comprehension of the story. She, a non-fisherwoman, would not let the author get away with fishing lingo without proper English. Even the striped bass would agree on the results of the work.

INTRODUCTION – PREFACE

There she was 30 years old, about my age, flaming red hair tucked under a salt stained long brimmed cap standing in the wash. About 5 foot 8 and even looking slim in those bloated rubberized waders. With one quick smooth whip of a 10 foot fiberglass rod she sent the Hopkins tin about 125 yards out. It was twilight about half an hour before sunset. Wind on shore about 15 knots, waves 4+ feet, sky cloudy, and air temperature in the 50s. For late October a good day for fishing. I knew the bass would be moving south and had to pass this point on the way to Virginia. I guess she knew the same. There were a few anglers north and south of us. We must be with a knowledgeable crowd who also knew the travels of the bass. It's rare to see a woman bass fishing from the surf at any time of the season. I just had to find out, "What are you doing here?" I slowly threw my AVA 27 to the left of me as I walked towards her position. Hoping I wouldn't get a strike, I kept it high in the water column.

As I approached her I was drawn by her quiet smile, porcelain complexion, blue eyes and of course her red hair. We started out talking about equipment and our season success before we introduced ourselves. Kate lived in the area but I wondered why I never saw her fishing here. The job for the government kept her more in the air than in the surf. Something with the government, not secret but in the industrial area. The more we talked I assumed she wasn't married. Her charm and beauty reminded me that this alone could scare young men from approaching her. She was well spoken and said it was required in her job. She said it was the business of using words, and the meaning of words.

We found a common interest between us, the striped bass. It brought our personalities to mesh like two different threads in the same fine linen. It was an interesting conversation encompassing local and national interests concerning the state of the striped bass. We fished together side by side for another hour, challenging each other to put the tins exactly where we wanted and joking about the frustrations in trying to lay the line evenly on the conventional reel and not get a bird-nest. Score over the hour, five nests for me and four for Katie. It was getting pretty dark by now so I suggested we have a bite to eat before I had to head to my next stop 75 miles up the coast. I said I was TC and told her about my radio, newspaper job and suggested a couple of spots to the north and south where she might find bigger bass. After dinner we parted, promising to meet about the same time and place a month later, if possible. It was a charming time. The hushing sound of the waves were overpowered by the zip of the line speeding off the Penn 150s. The sun was about now a red ball as it crept towards the horizon. It danced along the waves, getting weaker as it started to sink away waiting for another day. The breeze died down in concert with the falling sun. Stillness settled over the water and the land. Even the waves gave up their hushing sound and seemed to realize the day was done. They retreated getting ready for the next high tide and again to do battle with the stubborn sand. The sand clinging to the shoreline and the waves trying to claim more of it. A zero sum game. Sun, surf, stripers and the stirring beauty of life united similar people of common interests. Might we meet again?

So the past contact with Katie soon faded with the seasons. Summer rushed into fall, then the long, dreary winter and finally bass season started again. This went on for about five years. The thought of Katie never completely disappeared yet I continued to suppress the feeling of another chance meeting at the surf-line. The reports of surf fishing up and down the coast line and the radio gig kept me busy and focused on the jobs. I gave presentations about fun and clean living found in fishing versus the lore of the world with negative activities. The kids just needed someone to help them get started. A basic rod, reel, line and hooks. With the invention of the spinning reel, months of practice with a conventional reel wasn't necessary. In my day, the conventional reel was the only available reel. The art of casting was only achieved by practice. It was easy to be discouraged from surf fishing by continual birds' nests leading to frazzled nerves. Driving to the beach for a day of fishing could be the last day if you spend the whole time untangling fishing lines.

I even offered the Eagle Scouts to help them with their" fishing badge" by taking them to the beach for a day of fishing. One of the local sporting goods stores offered us a few surf rods, spinning reels loaded with line for the scouts. I supplied the terminal tackle and bait. I didn't expect them to catch much and they didn't. Competition focused not on the quantity of the catch but on the length of the cast. With saltwater fishing experience attained, the merit badge accepted, I expect these kids to reenact this day with their kids in years to come. I planted the seed and hoped it would sprout especially using saltwater environment as the prime ingredient.

The sequence of work and play was interrupted by the California Department of Fish and Games requests to confer with them about the striped bass conservation movement in the East Coast. The California Fish and Game had the official government statistical data but they wanted to know what the fishermen wanted in a conservation movement. I wondered what conservation movement they were talking about. It was more like a striped bass potential conservation movement was more political than conservational. One day the radio station got a call from NOAA. They wanted someone with extensive striped bass recreational fishing experience and contacts in the commercial part of the striped bass industry to aid California in developing a conservation program.

Late in the 1800s, striped bass were introduced to the northern California area. After time they were firmly established in the San Francisco Bay and San Joaquin River. Little knowledge was known about the activities at the local level of striped bass in these areas only estimates were available on the catch. Since striped bass was not considered a major fish in California and a foreign introduced species the present status was only partly known. Salmon, the natural species, was king.

The radio station received a financial package to cover the cost and both the radio station and my weekly fishing column. They thought it would be a good way to expand interests in other areas of the US. My radio broadcasts would be live and my fishing column would be weekly.

I jumped at the opportunity. I personally knew little about the California striped bass recreational and commercial activities. We decided on 5 days of working at the local tackle shops manufacturer of fishing products, a couple of meetings at the largest fishing clubs and a day at the Department of Fisheries in Sacramento. A day to travel to and from California would add up to about a week. With a radio broadcast from the associated stations and a phone call for fishing reports, it would be a busy week. From the anglers at the beaches and river, I would get a good picture of the striped bass situation. Could the East Coast anglers learn anything what to avoid or what to accept? Interesting, I will not have a rod, nor reel nor line but I would take a few of my most precious lures. This could be a two-way learning experience.

Two weeks later I was on my way to Sacramento, California. Department of Fisheries to discuss the East and West Coast striped bass situations.

The 1980s was probably the best years for the striped bass in California. Previously the commercial catch was at least 1,000,000 pounds until-1935 when it ceased in order to improve the recreational striped bass fishing. A striped bass fishing stamp led to $1.5 million (now dropped} for improvements including a certain portion for the salmon. Hatcheries were developed in order to increase the participation of the striped bass but since the state and federal waters diversion project took water from the waterways for farm purposes, the striped bass situation was in decline.

The fish reside in the San Francisco Bay area and moved to the Delta region to spawn about March. The Delta area comprises much land east of San Francisco and the San Joaquin River. The coastal surf fishing in the Bay, near Berkeley, south of the Bay, Marion beaches, San Mateo coast and Monterey Bay all the way to San Diego were active. In the inland area the fish prefer shad, blood worms, sardines, anchovies, pile worms and bull heads. Off the beach trolling with spoons, Hopkins lures and umbrella rigs produced results. By mid-June the bass were back in the Bay or along the coast. The financial impact of striped bass recreational fishing in northern California had been seriously reduced because of water quality and quantity in this spawning area. There is no commercial industry for striped bass. By law you cannot sell your catch.

I arrived at the California Department of Fish and Game early of the week. Of course I was 3 hours early, failing to change my bio clock as well as the one on my wrist. Not much to do in Sacramento in the early morning. Coffee shops are in tune with the movement of the state employees. Yesterday's newspapers kept me busy until the 7-8 and 9 AM crowds got activities rolling.

With contacts in the Department of Fisheries I found some knowledgeable and interested employees who knew about the striped bass. I received bits of info from a variety of people who always suggested another person could help me more. There was a striped bass table where a part time editor wrote about a conservation program for this species. I was to be introduced to her but today was not her working day. I notice a picture of a woman next to a 40+ pound striped bass caught in the San Francisco Bay a few years ago. Those fuzzy photos in the local paper could not clearly identify the fish as a striper nor the woman other than Ms. Woodward. Sorry I missed her but I left my card and asked her to call so we could discuss the striped bass situation in California. I suggested some sort of tagging program like the East Coast had might help her direct the conservation program.

I visited the Delta, marine docks, beaches and talked to tackle shops but all were more involved with other species of fish due to the decline of the striped bass numbers. They told me fish finder rigs, and hooks from 4/0 to 8/0 were common. Line/reels about the same as the East, 4 ounces' sinkers were standard but bait quite different. lures seem to be more of metal and plastic poppers, but bait the most popular presentation. The San Francisco Bay region and the San Joaquin Delta was quite large and it would take weeks to cover it and the coastal surf fishing area. The shops said there was active striped bass surf fishing. One of the officers in the Fish and Game Department just came back from a striped bass fishing trip on the Sacramento River. At $200 per person for 5 guys they caught stripers all day.

Much of my time was either in Sacramento, phone calls to the Department of Fish and Game or driving along the Delta region. The Delta is a wonderful place for fauna and flora. Boaters have innumerable places to fish for bass and salmon. Coastal boat anglers can do the same along the ocean coastline or in the region of the San Francisco Bay, Sacramento River and the San Joaquin River. The Bay area has a semi-saltwater environment while the further east you go the saltwater content is essentially zero. Here is where the water is sent to the south for agricultural use and there is talk about building a pipeline from the salt free Delta water to the south for the farmers. This would essentially be detrimental for the striped bass and salmon. Both contribute little to the GNP of California (less than 1%}. Agriculture contributes 2% of its GNP. Finance, insurance and real estate equal about 21%. Services and government equal about 13%. California's GNP is about $4 trillion.

Surprisingly someone from the California Striped Bass Association heard I was in town and gave me a call. The club of about 2000 members has 7 chapters in the region. It must be a striper club for they meet at C. K. Grill and Bar in Latrobe, California. They asked me to attend their monthly meeting. I told them I would like to but time did not allow it. We had a lengthy conversation via phone about the striped bass situation. Their position was that the increased movement of water to the southern farm areas was a major reason for the decline of striped bass. They said the adult bass population was about 4,000,000 in the 1960, 775,000 in 1990 and 300,000 today. Department of Fisheries estimate that there was 600,000 bass in 1995, 2,000,000 in year 2000. Today it was unknown.

Water has always been a problem for Californians. The agricultural industry requires 80% of available water but contributes a small amount to the $4 trillion GNP of the state. California's farms contribute $54 billion from 76,000 farms to its GNP. It's a tangled web of conflicting interests between government, private citizen and the co-op farmers of the south. The average rainfall of 26 to 38 inches was from the north, 13 to 20 from the central region, 18-33 from Sacramento and 6 to 13 from the San Joaquin Delta.

Water may flow downhill but dollars always flow to state capitals. So I got into the water problem up to my neck. The daily fishing reports came more from tackle shops, guides, etc. as well as Sacramento. The weekly radio show summarized most of the events of the week. I had a chance to scout along the coastal region were fishing was active but soon realized surf fishing was done from San Francisco Bay all the away to San Diego. Much too long to cover. The Striped Bass Association was trying to increase the striped bass population. The 2000 members were voting citizens and had a say in the political area of Sacramento. They are counterbalanced by the co-op farmers of the south willing to pay for more water. Income from fishing licenses cannot complete this zero sum game. Saltwater fishing consist mostly of 8 ½, foot to 12 foot rods, fish finders, big hooks and conventional sinkers. Baits were blood worms, sardines, anchovies, pile worms, herrings, shrimp and bull heads. Fishing season was all year. Fishing license was about $47 for one rod plus an additional $5.14 for 2nd rod. Ideal fishing temperature for bass was about 55'F. There was about 1,400,000 anglers buying fishing licenses. The popular fish caught along the surf was perch, striped bass, halibut, smelt, croaker and corbina.

It became obvious to me before concluding my trip that since the striped bass was not a natural resident fish in California; they don't want them here but they won't go away. It's on its own. This is the present position in Sacramento as best as I understand. This was my opinion based on the literature and speaking to the appropriate people. These decisions are usually made at the highest academic levels and passed down to the responsible government agencies.

This fight over water rights, water quality and water quantity has been going on for decades. It wasn't going to be resolved by me or any other earthly being. I left Sacramento for chance to spend some time in the Delta area. I drove around looking for fishermen some conversation. I saw them along the bank but from where I was on the road, I could not get down to the bank with my 9 to 5 attire. With my binoculars I noticed one Asian looking fishermen with 2 rods while sitting in his folding chair. One of the rod tips continuously moved to indicate there was fish there. This action continued with more action at the tip. Finally, he reeled in the line. Nearly a dozen small fish were attached to the long line full of hooks and bait. As he removed and gutted all the fish, there was action on the other rod. A later conversation with the Sacramento people confirmed this was not an uncommon event. One of the reasons there was an 18-inch minimum size for the striped bass was; get them young and often. They miss the often portion because there was a limit of two stripers per day.

I headed back to Sacramento to finish up my report, fishing news for the newspaper and prepare for the radio report. It was a quick, varied and upsetting visit. I thanked all for their help and my overall conclusion was the striped bass was an unwelcome fish in California by part of the scientific elite but not with the fishermen. Conservation efforts appeared to placate the fishermen. How things had changed from the late 1800.

I wonder if Washington DC would consider my conclusions.

CHAPTER 1

I didn't know him. My wife's uncle, TC, recently lost his wife and decided to move. They had a rinky-dinky cottage at the shore. As they aged they spent less and less time there but he still recalled good memories at the cottage. Johnny's Bait Shop and Joe's Bass Barn were his favorite haunts.

Johnny's Bait Shop was almost around the corner from TC's place. It was so close to the shore that during the storms sand piled up about one quarter the height of the cottage. Johnny shoveled the sand away but only from the front door. The sand made the place looked like pyramid that held secrets about fishing so no advertisement was needed. Johnny was a middle-aged happy guy with a wife and two kids. They did the fishing, he did the register. The place didn't look very big because fishing stuff hung from the walls and the bait was iced in the tub. You didn't have to worry about getting bait somewhere else. At 5 AM Johnny was already there and even hung around to 10 PM for the night crew. Easy-going and always with a smile Johnny made his living doing business here and there all season long but the bait/tackle shop was his favorite place. TC introduced me to him and we immediately connected when he said his wife retired from the U.S. Patent

Office some years ago. It was like meeting part of a similar family with like careers.

I told him about my wife's work as best I could and why my vacation started here. I said I was Ted, we shook hands and said we would be seeing him soon but probably not at 5 AM. That time is reserved for the 'can't sleep' surf jockeys.

Up the beach near the mini boardwalk was Joe's Bass Barn. Joe was much more serious than Johnny. He catered to the striper client. His shop was smaller than Johnny's big store but even more crowded with rods, reels and lures. If Joe didn't have what you wanted no one did. If you were going striper fishing here was the place to check in. An open book with the recent bass logged in lay on the counter. Date, time, lure/bait but not the location. Lots of surf jockeys would just call in with the info and not be confronted with questions where the bass were caught. The logbook was considered accurate. It was only a record of what bass were kept but not what were released. Since you could not legally keep more than two bass at 28 inches, you wouldn't know if a blitz was somewhere in the local area or anywhere in a cell phone contact area. Joe was an elderly and retired surf jockey who knew the soul of the bass. He could tell you season, place and tide when the bass could be found. I asked him a question about the bass and his reply was, "It depends." This comment would come up again and again. Later I recalled where it originated.

For me my fishing days phased out during the college years, then marriage called and then the baby cried. I never gave fishing much thought until my wife had to go to Europe for a few weeks. The tech company was holding seminars on the company's patents. With the competition in the high-tech area heating up, the company needed to make it. clear to the competition that her company would litigate those who use their patent unless they signed a license agreement. This was the real purpose of the trip, not to threaten but to sign up. The trip should last several weeks as they toured the major European capitals. If they were successful in Europe, they might extend the trip to the Far East. This could add at least another week. "What would I do for nearly a month?" I thought. Since she was taking a work related "vacation", I figured I would do the same and also give my condolences to the uncle as well as catch up on sun, sea and fishing.

I found it wasn't quite that easy. Top Cat or TC thought I, Ted, was one of those Internet news groups trying another sales approach. After reviewing the genealogy of our families with him, via phone, based on what little I knew, he confirmed I was part of the family tree. The conversation warmed up after that. He talked about his late wife who surprisingly was also a heck of a surfcaster. In the early autumn before the cold winds returned for their annual visit, you could catch her casting away with a 10 foot bamboo surf rod. She loaded the Penn model 155 Squidder reel with 175 yards of Cortland linen line. She was a committed and dedicated surf jockey even rinsing the linen with fresh water after each day's fishing. She was a sight to see with chest waders, ponytail hanging out of her salt stained cap and fancy ladies sunglasses. She was about 5 foot 10, 150 pounds with an athletic type body. Loading a bamboo rod with 3 ounces of tin was no problem for her. With her left foot firmly planted in the wash, she would lay about 4 or 5 feet of line perpendicular to the sand and then with one swift motion lay out the line and tin about 75 to 110 yards. She admitted she was not a perfect casting machine as one could see by the leather thong cover on her right thumb. Bird-nests were not uncommon events with the conventional reels. Although she was gone, TC could still picture her in the suds with her bloated waders, designer sunglasses and telephone pole bamboo rod.

The timing seemed right, my wife on her business trip, Top

Cat's loss, and urge to recall my past fishing experiences. A week later I drove to TC's cottage. Not the kind of place to hold formal dinners or upscale parties. I could hear the pounding surf as I approached the front door.

The 25' x 30' well weathered cottage reminded me of unpainted furniture. It needed a coat of weather beater paint, a few replacement roof cedar tiles, rain gutter realignment and a new Welcome sign on the front door, as only the 'well c …' part of the sign was left. It seemed to ask the question 'Well what do you expect after years of neglect." I knocked gently at the door fearful the cottage might not like to be disturbed from its summer slumber. TC opened the door and let me in. He was about 5 foot 10, wiry build, wearing seashore clothes.

A strong handshake told me he meant what he said and said what he meant. "You must be Ted", he said. "I'm glad we could get together."

His cottage was a museum of surf rods from 8 feet to 11 feet hung vertically from the ceiling all neatly aligned from the smallest upfront to the longest in the rear. From one wall hung two pairs of full chest waders, one rubber Red Ball, an unnamed rayon combo, various tins, and wooden plugs hung from a 360° shelving 7 feet above the floor all around the den. The den was about 80% of the cottage with a little room left for the kitchen, bedroom and toilet. A true seashore cottage most of the living area for relaxation, fun and fishing.

After the two minute tour of the place, TC invited me to a lunch of clam chowder and blackened striped bass. The French merlot wine poured into elegant stained wine glasses indicated Top Cat was more than his sea shore smile, an elegant gent living in a well-worn wooden shack.

After lunch we took a walk down to the surf. The wind was

from the west about 5 to 10 knots, tide seemed to be rising, with a light chop and the wave height about 2 to 3 feet.

I asked him," How does it look for fishing?"

TC said, "It depends."

"Depends on what?" I said.

TC said, "The tide, wind direction and speed, water temperature, chop and wave height."

"Well," I said, "That doesn't help me."

"Maybe," TC said, "You ought to ask what fish you are after."

I said, "Lets' say I want to bottom fish in the surf for whatever's running in the summer." "Okay," TC said." Without being specific about a particular species, let's start with the most common bait that most bottom fish would eat, clams."

"That sounds good," I said. "I know how to handle them, hook them up and wait." Top Cat commented that he was glad I recalled my early years of surf fishing. "Yes," I said, "And I also recall that fresh clams are a must unless frozen is the only available option."

Top Cat congratulated me in knowing fresh bait is mandatory for all bottom feeders such as kingfish, bass, weakfish, cod, redfish and flounder to name a few. In a similar way fresh or frozen squid is also tops on their menu along with sand and bloodworms. A chunk of bunker has been known to lure striped bass as other game fish but less so for ground fish.

"Have any terminal tackle ideas for these ground fish?" I asked.

"Ted let's start with what's in the water," replied TC

Big hooks from 9/0 for big fish and under 1/0 for others. There are many brands. Choose hooks with coated steel or all stainless. Most important is sharpness. Dull hooks bring fishing stories to a "What happened" end. Another surprising end is when the bass roll at the surf-line and throws the hook. Lower your rod. Upright rods at this time will pull the hook out. Keep your hook sharpening bar hung around your neck to remind you it's always "hook sharpening time". Learn a knot or two to tie your hooks, leaders and line. Don't try to learn the great variety of knots available. In the middle of the night or on a cold morning, get your fingers and mind to recall the 1 or 2 knots, not all the others you barely remember. Fumbling fishing line in the cold weather is losing time, fishing time.

Essentially mono leaders work well. No need to exceed 20 to 40 pounds or 2-3 feet in length. Remember mono can stretch to 25% so you don't want a long delay after the bite to the strike. Shorter length is better except for abrasive shorelines. Mono will better resist rocky bottoms with mono leaders than braid away your braided fishing line.

TC asked, "Ted, what leader material do you use?"

"I don't remember. Does it make a difference?"

"It depends," was TC's reply. "Thank God made the acuity of fish's eyes less than ours. It is approximately three times less but it differs with species of fish; the carp is the worst or about 15 times less acuity than us. Use the least visible leader with the best tensile strength for the job, else the fish might see your offering."

I asked," What's new in leader materials?"

"Try fluorocarbon which mimics the refraction of ocean water," he replied. I asked, "TC what else should I know about bait fishing?"

"It depends on the weather, tide, ocean temperature etc.," he said.

"Well give me a hint," was my reply.

TC replied, "In general if you have 5+ foot waves, you'll need 8 ounces of lead to hold bottom, with wind over 20 knots, and ocean water temperature below 50° F, stay home-*unless the bass are there.*"

I asked about terminal tackle again. TC said for the ground fish, keep it simple, the sinker on the bottom of the rig and two short leaders above with barbed hooks. For game fish like bass use a fish finder rig.

"What's a fish finder rig?" I questioned. "Does it really find fish, if so why don't we use it all the time?"

"It depends," he said, "Another depends?" I replied.

TC said, "The fish finder allows the fish to swim away with the bait without resistance from the drag discs in the reel. Some fish with bony mouths may approach the bait with caution and be lured to the hook via this approach. I remember a day in the surf when I had walked away from my rod to talk to another surf jockey. I had the Shimano bait caster reel on the no drag mode with the fish finder rig as my terminal tackle. I had the head of a bunker tied to a 7/0 hook. When I returned to my rod I noticed a big bow in the line. There wasn't enough wind to cause this, hence the fish must have picked it up. So I slowly reeled in the line to get rid of the bow and set the reel to the drag mode. Then set the hook. Well, all I did was pull the bunker head out of the mouth of the bass. It wasn't crab season nor shark environment. Probably a small bass hoping to grow big enough to swallow the head. I got the head back in good shape. The name of the hook identifies the shape of the hook."

"What's next?" I asked.

"Depends. Let's say sinkers."

"What's so important about them?"

Top Cat followed, "It depends on many things. On a regular day with moderate surf conditions, a conventional 4 ounce lead sinker, pyramid or oval, should hold bottom for you. If for some reason you must fish in high surf conditions with bait and not lures, surfers have used up to 8 ounces of lead. Even the "parachute" sinker can be used to secure the bottom. Beyond 8 ounces is better to leave bottom fishing for another day. You can expect to have a rough day using 8 plus ounces, strong winds, fast currents, white water wave action, stirring up seaweed etc."

"Well that sounds like unreasonable fishing conditions." was Ted's reply. "Any reason to use particular hooks?" he asked.

Yes, TC came right back to me. "The circle hooks will catch more fish and can release them without injury. There are various sizes and shapes of circular hooks but they mostly all work the same way by hooking the fish on the side of the mouth. In fact it is claimed the fish will hook itself most of the time. I can't swear to this because I've never seen a fish hook itself but it's probably true. The "J" hook and its variations can get to the deep innards of the fish, hence its release is nearly impossible without serious injury."

"Now since we have covered sinkers, hooks what else do I need?" I interrupted. "I was used to the old Cortland linen then mono line. Which do you prefer?"

"Neither," TC said. "Although the braided-like line was available in the 1950s, it recently has been exclaimed as the' must use' fishing line. Good advertisement in the past for all other lines, tied the braided line in 'knots'. In fact although it is about four times smaller in diameter than mono line at the same tensile strength, making a secure knot can be a problem. The braided line has a low friction surface hence knots can come undone unless carefully tied. This low friction surface allows surfcasters and all other fishermen, salt and freshwater, to cast bait/lures farther than all other fishing lines. To prevent backlashes, and we haven't found the no-backlash line material yet, you need a steady force on the spool to keep the line laying evenly. This is for both conventional reels with revolving spools as well as spinning reels. The smaller diameter of braided line, the more susceptible to fouling. Light line can dig into the line already spooled; it can also loop around the outside of the spool unless you have residual force on the line. With the aid of a sinker you have a residual force on the line as you retrieve. Using lures with spinning reels, you must be careful to keep the line on the spool before starting the retrieve. With the conventional reel the line is always on the spool, not so with the spinning reel. To avoid this potential problem with the spinning reel, most surfcasters manually close the bail wire by hand. This avoids looping of the loose line on the spool and around the spool. Penn's 706 spinning reel removed the bail wire. Putting the line on the line roller is the only option.

Be aware braided line tends to fray more than mono line and is more visible to the fish. Hence mono line is usually used as leader material where hooks and sinkers are attached. All are attached to a common joint by a swivel including the braided fishing line. Some perfectionist using 10 pound test braided will tie the line directly to the lure. One less connection, one less problem. Avoid wrapping your fingers, hand, wrist around braided line unless you want to lose one of them. Braided line cuts very well and party boat captains often do not allow braided line on their boats. It has the potential to slice into plastic hulls. Motoring to port with half a boat and half the passengers is not good for business."

"Oh, I got that; line, leader, sinker, hooks and the swivel which ties all together. What's next?" I asked Top Cat.

"Depends," he said. "Got time for the variation of surf rods, bay rods, and jetty rods for bait fishing and lures?"

"Sure you bet," I said.

TC said," Okay. Depends how tall you are. At 5 1/2 a 12 foot rod will be too tall for you and at 6 ft. 4, a 10 foot rod would be too small. An average height surfer should be able to handle 10 foot rod either for bait or lures. Back in the old days we only had bamboo rods. A 9 foot- 10 foot rod was all you had. It seemed to weigh 3 to 5 pounds and handle like a baseball bat. With ferrules, rope-like line, guides, reel clamp and reel, the whole contraption probably weighed more than 3 pounds. Try casting this system all day with lures. Better to be a weight lifter than a white-collar worker. That brings us to materials used in fishing rods. For salt or freshwater, they can be the same materials.

Bamboo was the material for the common surf rod in the early 1900s. Ted, you ought to read Charles B. Church's story about his world record 73 pound bass in 1913. His record bass was surpassed by AI McReynolds 78.5 pound bass caught in 1982. You do not need high tech equipment to catch big fish. Church with his bamboo rod and German silver fishing reel and McReynolds with his relatively old rod and Penn 710 spinning reel with the 20 pound test mono line, confirmed it.

Bamboo was still the rod material till the 1950s. I remember the HarLee Company, Jersey City, New Jersey offered a black fiberglass rod blank. From my money working after school at the old A&P grocery store, I purchased one. Adding the accessories butt, guides and reel holder, the 10 foot rod saw action up and down the New Jersey coast until college called. For sheer power fiberglass can hold its own even today with carbon fiber rods. Of course the fiberglass rods were not much lighter than bamboo and they were about as indestructible as today's lightweight carbon tube wrapped with carbon cloth. The art of casting with bait or lures has to be learned no matter the rod materials."

"Well TC what do you recommend?"

"It depends," he said. "You can choose among well- known rod builders. Cost and availability is a factor. You may also want to have a custom rod built to fit your physical build and you can decorate it with your own color scheme. There is an ideal rod for every situation."

"What do you mean?" I asked." I have to buy a rod for every surf condition, jetty situation, back-bay or salt water creek?"

"Could be."

"Please explain this?" I barked back.

"It depends," again TC said. "Now for bait fishing, where you want to place the bait on the bottom of the ocean, bay, creek or wherever, almost any rod will do. You should choose a rod compatible for the fish you seek. You wouldn't use an 11 foot surf rod in a creek nor a 6 foot rod in this surf. Balance is the key to success. A light 7-8 foot rod for kingfish in the surf will do as well for snapper blues in the bay. Putting bait on the bottom is easy, putting a lure in the right water column is another matter. Rod, reel, line and lure all must be considered as well as wind, tide, water conditions and wave action."

I asked, "TC how can one possibly choose among all these conditions and options?"

He replied, "Let's finish up with the bait situation. You have the correct rod for the size of the quarry, carbon fiber material preferred in the 9 to 12 foot range. Choose a spinning reel of your preference holding up to 300 yards of 20-30 pound test braided line. Always look for structure along the beach to hold fish. Deep water for daylight fishing, shallow water for evening fishing. If you can cast to the last wave from the shoreline, which may be hundreds of yards out, that's where many fish would be feeding on clams, worms, sand fleas and trapped baitfish. There will be several smaller sandbars reroute to the beach where waves will produce white water as waves break over them. The last wave falling on the beach may be the best one if you can't get to the one far off the beach. As the last wave falls on the beach, its water recedes back into the surf. This rush of water disrupts the subsurface exposing all kinds of fast fish food, like a drive-in at McDonald's or Burger King. It's there for the pickings and swept away in the next backwash. Fish know this, do you?"

"I heard that jetties and groins are good places to fish, maybe better than the surf," I said?

"Ted, it depends on a lot of things, TC replied. First you better have a strong rod. Something that can haul the fish up the rocks."

I replied. "How am I going to cast a lure with a telephone-pole rod?"

"Again it depends on the rod. It is okay for bait fishing from the rocks but you have to compromise for a semi casting/lure rod for the rocks. Many jetty jocks will have a 4 to 10 foot gaff with them on the rocks, hence they are not too concerned about getting the fish up. A stout fishing line of 30 to 40 pounds can only offer you some confidence that you have a fair chance of landing the fish. So you see, it's a balance of rod, reel, line and bait/lure and again depends on the balance with these fishing tools. Don't forget your shoes, "TC barked out.

"What do you mean, TC?"

"Never go on the rocks without cleated boots. Seaweed, moss, crustaceans, slime will do you in if you fall on or in the rocks or in the water. Secondly, always go on the rocks with a fishing buddy or at least with other rock jocks already there. It is the best insurance you can have in an emergency. If you know one pile of rocks well, the right steps to take, at the right tide, right moon and right time, you should succeed. Good luck and keep your cell phone dry."

"All right TC, you covered bait fishing with rod, reel, line, and terminal tackle from the beach, rocks in good and bad weather. What's left?" I asked.

"Well it depends on your eyesight," TC replied.

"You're kidding," was my reply.

"It is the water you have to dissect, was his reply. All things being equal dark water means deeper water. These fish tend to reside there after they have scoured the shallow waters for food. Ambushing is always more successful if you can hide out of sight. So casting to deep water is probably a good place to start."

"If I can determine the deep waters what do I do?"

TC said, "The very best thing you should do is to check the beach at low tide not high tide.

If you are new to the area, this is the key to successful catching not just fishing. Sandbars, subsurface structures and holes will be visible. These can be most visible during full and new moon strong tide cycles especially in the early spring. Your scouting time will be well rewarded. If you miss scouting at low tide hang around other local fishermen who had already done their homework. Be aware that after winter storms, the subsurface structure may have changed. A notepad with the landmarks highlighted is a good idea, if you fish other beaches. This will profit you, if you fish with lures. Fish tend to locate where they can ambush prey. Holes, sandbars and rocks are where you want to cast your lures. Exception is where you see birds diving for fish. Let them show you where the baitfish are and possibly the game fish. An old friend of mine once said "This was for tourists". He meant put your time-in and find where the holes, sandbars and rocks are located. Be a real educated surf jockey. Either way take advantage of what is offered; don't be a perfectionist.

Don't expect many swimming bait fish in the early spring. The water is still cold and the baitfish will arrive with warmer waters somewhere north of 50°. Scouting the beach will always be your best option for better fishing from spring to autumn. Fishing with lures should be coordinated with the arrival of baitfish: bunker, mullet, spearing, sand eels and juvenile sport fish. I've seen bluefish chase 4 to 6 inch weakfish right on the beach. All fish can be baitfish depending upon size of the predators."

"Okay, can I use the bait rod for lure fishing?" I asked?

"Depends," TC replied. "If you are fishing from a bridge or a place where lifting the fish from the water may be a problem with a light casting rod and you are using a lure in the 3-6 ounce range, a bait rod will be your best bet. Be sure your line, leader, terminal connections can handle the weight of the fish. Night fishing from bridges can be rewarding as well as work. One of my friends had a contraption that when the fish was hooked, he lowered the clamping device attached with a slip ring around his fishing line and lowered it down to the head of the fish which was held just above water. The device had its own 100 pound rope tied to it. As the device hit the head of the fish, the teeth opened up around the head. The teeth dug into the head as the fisherman pulled on the cord. This way all of the weight of the fish was held by the 100 pound test cord not the fishing line as the slip ring guided the fish up the fishing line. He believed he lost a record bass due to a poor knot or line. This was not a catch and release device. It was a hook and land device. I think that concludes using bait rods with lures."

"What is your recommendation for rod, reel and line for surf fishing with lures?" I asked. "It depends," barked TC. "With a bait rod, reel and line all you need is to cast the bait to a spot in the surf. A spot where you probably located when you walked the shoreline at low tide. But with a casting rod using lures, you have many options in size, manufacturers and materials."

"What size do you recommend, TC?"

"Aside from the fact that there is a perfect rod for each condition of wind and surf, it depends on the weight of the lure you want to use. One to 3 ounces would handle well with a 9 to 10 foot carbon fiber rod. You'll find the recommendation weight of the lures usually on a decal near the lower one third of the rod. For lures in excess of 3 to 6 ounces, an 11 to 12 foot rod would do better, if you can handle that size rod. Experience says you should be 6 foot+ to handle these long rods. Don't discard glass fiber rods for either bait or lure fishing when you are casting heavyweight baits or 6 ounce lures. These rods are very powerful for holding big, heavy fish. Modern carbon rods with exotic materials are light and strong."

"TC, you have talked about rod, reel, line and fishing with lures but what kind of lures? You mentioned materials like wood and plastics. I see some of the wooden plugs that are so beautiful who would dare use them? They are like artwork."

"Don't be fooled by their beauty. If they swim and look like a fish, they could be worth the price of their beauty. Be aware striped bass eyes are most sensitive to the color light green; which is approximately the same color as their favorite bait fish- bunker. The total light spectrum of striped bass is similar to human eyes. There are a variety of fishing plugs that catch bass. I don't want to tell you to use certain shape plugs under certain conditions, there are books written about this matter. Bass will feed on mostly anything that swims. They will be attracted to the surface with pencil poppers, floating swimmers, regular poppers, bottle necks, atoms and a variety of other top water swimming plugs. In a similar way, striped bass will feed on baitfish that swim under the surface, which is imitated by sub-surface swimming plugs, soft baits, sand eel plugs and a variety of metal tins like Hopkins and similar metals. Bass spend a lot of time foraging the bottom sand especially for the leftovers by bluefish. Yet metal sand eel lures, bucktails and rigged eels attract bass swimming near the ocean bottom. Beauty in artificial lures only has value if they catch fish. Even without color, motion, noise, or smell, ugly top water and subsurface plugs can catch fish.

So at about 5 ft.10, try a 10ft. rod to handle 1 to 3 ounces of wood, soft plastic or metal. Rods of 11 to 12 feet need heavy lures but you better be 6 foot plus and able to load the rod (having the rod compress). In order to cast lures well you must choose the right weight lure for the conditions of wind, tide, and wave action. If the lure cannot load the rod, your casting distance will be reduced. Remember there is usually a perfect rod for the right situation but who can afford a dozen rods at $100-$300 each. Your one or two rods will be a compromise. If you happen to surf fish North Carolina or South Carolina coastline, surf jockeys need to get well off the beach with their presentation. You will find rods in the 12 to 15 foot range as the necessary tools for long, long casts. There are occasions in North Carolina when long or short rods cannot be used. In the fall around Thanksgiving time bluefish migrate south with the baitfish past Chesapeake Bay and head to North Carolina. I have been told by good friends that when bluefish thrash baitfish along the shoreline for as far as you could see, you cannot throw any lure in the water. If you did, the line would be immediately cut by the massive amount of bluefish. No rod of any size could hook up and hold a fish. What a sight that must have been.

Now that I have helped you select the general purpose fishing rod, what kind of reel can you handle?" TC asked.

"What do you mean?" I asked, "Conventional or spinning?"

TC commented, "The conventional reel as the old standard Penn 140 or 150, has a spool that rotates with the line as you cast. The line and spool become one unit in motion. An experienced surf caster will outdistance another using a spinning reel. One of the negative parts of the conventional reel is the backlash. If the line is not evenly laid on the spool, it is quite possible the spool will spin faster than the release of the line. If the line backs up on the spool, the well-known and dreaded backlash or birds-nest results. In the daylight it is easier to untangle; in the dark it is better to have another reel loaded with line.

The conventional surf reel will be needed to get to the sandbar that is usually out of reach by other reels. There are conventional surf reels that have a line guide which uniformly lays line on the spool. By increasing drag by the line guide, you reduce your casting distance and the common backlash, most of the time. For those just starting or renewing surf casting, the conventional reel is the most difficult to learn. Timing when to release your thumb off the spool will be difficult with different weighted lures and rod flex. Once you master the technique, your thumb will be an educated piece of equipment. Old souls and women use a thumb shield. After a while, if you are not using reels with a line guide, you learn to lay the line properly on the spool. Men were proud of the scarred thumbs while women had no qualms using the leather shields. Those less educated went to the line guide reel; lost distance but they saved their tender thumb."

I asked TC if he suggested I go with the other reel, the spinning reel. "It depends," was his common answer. "Spinning reels are not immune from birds-nest. If the line rests loosely on the spool, the next cast may cause the birds-nest. Braided line is likely used with spinning tackle. The line is about four times smaller in diameter than mono line at the same tensile strength, therefore you can put much more line on the reel. Birds-nest are more difficult to untangle with the smaller diameter line and they tend to lump together if the line is loosely retrieved. Two or more spare spools are the answer to the situation. The best way to avoid birds-nest with spinning reels is to have continued tension on the line. By manually closing the bail wire after the cast, you avoid loose line hanging off the spool, loose line hanging around the reel and loose line looped around the drag control. There is nothing more frustrating than a tangle of small diameter braided line at night. Be smart by manually closing the bail wire and check if the line is laying on the spool. Some spinning reels are manufactured without a bail wire hence forcing you to place the line on the line roller. If you prefer fishing at night go with the "no bail wire" option. You absolutely do not want a birds-nest on a spinning reel especially if you are a perfectionist using 10 pound braided line. This braided line finds a way into and around places on the spool where it shouldn't be. Bigger diameter braided line tends to reduce these chances."

"What about getting seawater in conventional or spinning reels?" I asked TC.

"It depends, some adventurous surf jockeys will put on waders or rubberized swimsuits and swim out to the rocks they can't reach casting from shore. This will often submerge rod, reel and line. Several reel manufacturers offer water-tight reels. If it is only saltwater you are concerned about, most all conventional and spinning reels can live in that environment, especially if you rinse them after each day's use. If sand is the problem no regular conventional or spinning reel will work for long in that environment. Try dropping the reel on the sand or swim with it submerged in a sand filled water area. This calls for a water-tight saltwater reel. Does this guarantee perfect operation of the reel? Ask the sandman how long can he be deterred.

Load reels to near capacity because after each day's fishing you should cut about 3-5 yards off the line which was subjected to the abrasive sand, rocks and often sub surface structures. This goes for either conventional or spinning reels. By loading the reel to near maximum capacity you increase your ability to cast farther since more of the line leaves the spool with less resistance. About an eighth of an inch is the suggested space between the top of line and the top rim of the spool. More is not good, less is better.

The when, how and where to use the equipment we talked about cannot be perfectly taught by me or anyone else. Experience is the only teacher. Yes read the good books, remember the best fishing tips, walk the beach, look where fish might hide, evaluate tide, current, wave action, wind direction and speed. If you see an old, salty fisherman with a frayed baseball cap sitting on an old bait bucket next to his surf rod, sit down in the sand next to him and admire his carefully chosen equipment for the present situation. Don't ask him for his secrets but about the most favorable environment needed to catch fish on this beach. You may not get the answer you want or you may get an answer you don't understand. Gary Player, the great golfer in the 1970s and 90s once asked Ben Hogan, another great golfer, about how to hit a golf ball. Hogan was one of the very best strikers of the ball. Gary wanted a tip on how to do it. Hogan's answer was to "dig it out of the dirt", that is; practice, practice, and practice. You may find the same answer from the old salt that is; put your time in the surf. Learn from your mistakes of poor timing, wrong tide, wrong moon, or wrong bait/lure. Your notebook about the seasons may be more valuable describing the bad fishing days than the successful ones. Fish species tend to be driven by their DNA, hence each species repeats their habits from one season to another. Scribe their habits in your note-book the where-when-how. Master chess champions often say they recall similar positions of the chess pieces of past games and can foresee the movements many more moves ahead. A good notebook should contain the probable movement of the fish, the where, when and how to exploit the situation.

Now you know about the tools let's go down to the beach and scout around."

"Okay", I said. "OJT is something I need to imprint in my brain the multi-mental and physical tasks needed to be a successful fisherman. Since I have a month until my wife returns from her business trip, what success should I expect?"

TC looked at me and said, "Ted, about zero, if you're lucky, zero plus. He continued, you will learn something each time you come out here. Check your notebook, plan what to take, plan where to go. You will be more successful than the uninformed angler hoping for a lucky day."

As we walked along the beach TC pointed out breakers on the offshore sandbars about 150 to 400 yards out. I watched as the waves broke on either side of the invisible sandbar. These passageways permit the fish to move into the inner portion of the beach. Here is where you hope for action even if you can't get your presentation to the sandbar. Since sandbars are not uniformly located at a set distance from the shoreline, scout the area at low tide.

As we continued to stroll along the beach, TC pointed at an array of empty clam shells scattered along the shoreline. Something had a feast on these clams and it probably was the fish at that sandbar about 150 yards out. Some of these clams rolled along the sand until they got caught in that last wave that crushed the clams in the trough a few yards off the shoreline or at the outer sandbar. You can bet the game fish will be at either place at early light, twilight and in the dark. Clam shells are also a good indication of clean water.

In a pinch for bait and in clean water look for sand fleas right at the shoreline. If you see a V formed by the receding wash, there are your sand fleas. About 1 inch long they lived in the region of the surf eating microscopic sea life. Game fish that frequent the shoreline will eat these tidbits especially those fish that don't mind getting their nose in the sand; striped bass, redfish, weakfish. A string of sand fleas on a 1/0 to 5/0 hook is a pretty good meal especially if the string holds 6 to 10. Easy pickins'.

Farther down the beach we see a rock pile that used to be a groin or jetty. TC indicated that such formations are homes for all kinds of sea creatures. Great place to hide for baitfish, variety of crabs, small clams, mussels, lobsters, juvenile game fish and ground fish. While standing on the shore, a cast parallel to the rocks may be the best way to cover more productive territory than to climb on the rocks and chance an injury. Summer flounder are known to locate in the sand next to the rock pile. A bucktail with a trailing skirt will prove the point during June and July.

By August they will start to move out. If you can persevere to autumn and the season is still open, the big boys will be looking for that bucktail. Unfortunately each state has its own season for size and limits which differ for commercial and recreational fishermen. Commercial boats usually harvest smaller fish and in greater numbers.

As we walked to the rock pile we noticed a jetty jock working at the end of the point. With full chest waders and baseball cap snug on his head, we could see the "Korker's" strapped to his boots. The metal spikes indicated he had the basic safety equipment. With a 10 foot medium flex carbon rod he looked like a conservative jetty jock. We quietly wished him good luck as we continued down the beach. Nearing the low tide mark TC pointed out a sandbar about halfway out to the major breakers. He suggested you could walk there before the next tide cycle and cast your bait or lure toward the big breakers. That's where the fish are. You may only have an hour or two before you have to move out or get caught in the deeper water as the tide fills in between sandbar and the shoreline. Know the water depth at low and high tide in your area.

TC said, "Let's go back to my place and have a snack, then we can talk about other matters about fishing." The snack turned out to be a multi-hour affair. The Bordeaux flowed freely, the bourbon glazed striped bass, clam chowder with real clams, seaweed with garlic sauce and Remy Martin as a chaser. This fisherman really knew how to fill body and spirit with good things. By now it was getting towards twilight and I felt like lights out was not too far away but it's not polite to fall asleep on your host after the first day.

We rose from the table, a forced move, and headed down to the beach again. The moon was about to rise. This gave me a chance to ask TC about its influence on fishing.

TC said, "It depends on experience more than rumor. For instance some fishermen have great luck during full moon and

21

new moon. Others have better luck a day or two before both. So experience seems to be the deciding factor. There is no guarantee that a surface popper during a full moon phase is easy to see by a game fish. New moon phase tends to entice fish to move to shallow water since the night will be all dark. Remember vision, sound, smell and motion are basic senses of fish. Deep water fish, where light is attenuated, use other sensors to locate food. Ground fish focus on smell and vision. Sound and motion of crustaceans, clams, mussels, worms etc. have little amplitude hence are of little value to ground fish. For game fish the opposite is needed for successful forage that is; vision, sound, smell and motion. Game fish tend to be found in water less than 100 feet where most bait fish swim yet big game fish can be found to 1500 feet. Most all game fish move to the surface to pursue their food. Medium sized game fish don't have the power to swim to the deep part of the ocean nor an air bladder to sustain the water pressure. Clams, mussels, sea worms, sand fleas and shrimp have a better chance of survival in the shallow near-shore waters. Tide, moon and water temperature control the environment of these near-shore fish. The rising water temperature draw baitfish, provide microscopic food for clams, mussels, sand fleas etc. Clams, crabs and mussels are at the top of the food chain of most shallow water fish.

Light is made up of many colors and fish see colors. That's one of the ways of finding food. Some scientists believe they see black and white yet their retinas with rods and cones means they have the capacity to see colors. You won't find evidence about what colors cod, blackfish, flounder, porgies, grouper or other ground fish see. It seems these ground fish depend more on smell for locating food. Game fish such as, striped bass, redfish, bluefish and weakfish need vision as the primary source to locate baitfish as their food although only one of these game fish, the striped bass, has been shown to have maximum sensitivity to light green color. The baitfish which striped bass fish feed on menhaden have skin with about the same color-light to medium green. It might be assumed that other game fish have color sensitivities for baitfish they seek. Each species is equipped to exploit its environment. Feeding below 1000 feet water depth, echo locating supersedes smell and vision."

Further down the beach I picked up an old, worn cap. One that you would normally see at a baseball game or just something to keep the sun out of your eyes. TC said, "That fisherman will have to get another one to increase his chances for success." I said, "A cap is a cap, what's so important?" TC said, "It has a long visor, adjustable strap, holes around the top of the cap and made of light denim material. The long brimmed cap allows your eyes even without sunglasses to keep sunlight from not only your eyes but cheekbone and other facial skin. A perfect material would be a shiny aluminum to reflect 90% of the sun rays. You will look like a tin man. You need contrast of colors in order to see changes in the ocean. Athletes use charcoal to help them see different colors by absorbing sunlight before the sun reflects into their eyes. Here is the surf caster in the 22nd century; a light weight metal helmet, charcoal covered eye sockets, zoom in sunglasses with magnification for night fishing. These fish won't stand a chance, most of the time."

I asked TC, "What kind of tackle bag should I get?"

He said, "It depends on what kind of fishing you intend to do. Bait or lures? A bait tackle bag should have lots of pockets. One for sinkers, hooks with leaders, swivels, pliers, hook removal tool, knife to open clams and cut bait, flashlight, extra spool with line, if possible, towel, scale, flexible ruler, stringer line, sunscreen, band aids, wire leaders, light to attach to rod for night fishing, a pocket for a sandwich, and a cell phone in a plastic pouch. Don't leave home without your lucky charm and a prayer to your fishing god. PS: Save a pocket at the last minute for something you will forget to take.

For short stays of 1 to 2 hours, just have rod, reel, bait, knife and cell phone. For all day affairs, take the kitchen sink plus a pail to sit on. In today's complex world of saltwater fishing, you may be wise to carry, if necessary, your saltwater national license, state license updated, supplement licenses for additional species, auto license with picture of you if you are an out of state angler. Be sure that you have no traffic citations outstanding. Most states now talk to each other, you may miss the good tide while paying the fishing license fine or traffic fine after the lifeguard leaves the beach and it's open to you. Remember the low tide mark identifies the limit of the property line for the residence on his sea shore property. The owner may own the sand on the beach but not the water. Some seashore townships have no access roads to the beach hence protecting the property ownership to the waterline depends on the violation. It is interesting that in some states after severe storms along the coast, the federal government along with the seashore townships, wanted to replenish the beach with additional sand. They needed the permission of the property owners to access their beach. Other townships without this restriction had access and the beach replenishing procedure went well. The owners of the restricted property said no. After the next coastal storm they had less sand hence beach to restrict. Ho-hum! States are trying to limit these transfer rights as the property is sold.

Such activity is present in the New England waters, Cape Cod, Vineyard, Block Island, Nantucket, New Jersey, etc.

Now getting back to your question about fishing rods, The minimum tackle for the plug fanatics surf jockeys and they all are, is rod, reel, line and his favorite lures of metal, wood and plastic in its various forms. On Long Island, New York it's the bucktail. Rigged eels, are good everywhere as well as sand eel in metal as

AVA's or in plastic/wood. Otherwise a bag hung over your shoulder with at least a half a dozen slots for other favorite lures will do. As the season changes and baitfish move from spring to summer to autumn, you can alter the mix. Make sure the bag has holes in the bottom to get rid of the water. The top cover should overlap the top a few inches. Waterproofing surf bags materials can be purchased at the local hardware store in a spray can. If you don't mind carrying around a water soaked surf bag all day, forget the waterproofing. As you work the beach be sure to have about 10 feet of plastic cord attached to the bag as your stringer. You don't want to pick up-drop-pick up your catch. The stringer will allow you to float catch along the shoreline. Don't forget a little plastic bag with swivels, leader, and a small multi use tool. Top yourself with the baseball cap, polarized sunglasses and sunscreen."

I asked TC if I needed a bowtie with my baseball cap.

He said," In the late autumn a turtleneck sweater could be the equivalent of a well formed bowtie and do a better job. Spring, summer, or autumn may be reason to vary your fishing clothing. Spring and autumn may require full length lightweight waders with a waist belt. Warm underwear should vary with outdoor temperatures, wind and weather forecasts. Not too many of us want to whirl away at noontime in the blazing sun of summer with the wrong equipment. Except for bluefish, other game fish may be best met in the predawn and early evening twilight. Such times with water temperatures in the mid-70s to mid-90s, something more than being naked may serve you best. Waders, shorts, sandals, T- shirt may be all you will need. Bug spray may be your best friend in midsummer if the onshore breeze is near zero and the temperatures near seasonal highs. Korkers all the time on the rocks in all season.

Breathable clothes are a must especially as you add more clothing as the cooler weather approaches. Technology has not only found its way in rod materials and fishing lines but also into space age clothing. Big baits, big lures get big fish, while lightweight clothing gives you the endurance to track the shoreline searching for your prey." "Is that about all for clothing?" I asked. "It depends," TC explained. "As your clothing changes with the seasons and your fishing tools of rod, reel, line and bait/lure vary, being comfortable gives peace of mind, body and spirit."

I asked TC if he traveled much in search of top surf fishing ventures.

TC said he was offered the job writing about his surf fishing experiences, I did travel for weeks at a time. My wife was tolerant of my travels, but it was considered sport by me not work. When the job offer came my wife was strongly against it because I would be gone and gone and gone again. Not healthy for a marriage unless she could come with me.

With her patent research job, it was not possible. My local radio and fishing column, required me to travel locally. I made a lots of friends in my work for the company. I had to keep up with changes in fishing regulations and seasons, increase minimum size, limited quota and the changing political atmosphere in Washington DC. Important changes about striped bass have occurred in Massachusetts where over 1 million pounds of striped bass were allowed to be caught by gentlemen and commercial fishermen. A gentleman commercial fisherman, was a fishermen who purchased a commercial license before the season opens, and fished during the season after a regular job. You were allowed to harvest striped bass until the quota of 1 million pounds was harvested. It was a way to make a few extra dollars. You could sell the bass to a licensed fish dealer, pocket the bucks, and maybe pay no taxes on the income especially if records of the pounds of stripers were not recorded. Some even went to Connecticut with their commercial catch of bass to get better prices. This avoids the pounds being recorded towards the Massachusetts quota. Recently over 3000 licenses were sold in Massachusetts, fewer than 10% reported their catch. Total poundage? Who knows?

YouTube reported hundreds of dead striped bass floating in the ocean claimed as "by catch" or discards. Being not part of the intended catch and not having a commercial license for the bass, they were released. If the commercial fishermen netted the favorite food of the bass, bunker also called menhaden, would you not expect the bass in the same vicinity? This probably goes up and down the East Coast and maybe elsewhere. Don't forget the cheaters. Not too long ago, 600,000 pounds of illegal striped bass was seized by Maryland and federal agents. Who knew how long this was going on? You can't have the federal or state agents at each marina on each day, week and month of the season and especially during off-season. Pilferers always have their own seasons using smaller boats, out of the way places and sell to markets who have their eyes, ears and mouth closed. They sell in secret and at night and slip away to do it again.

I asked TC, "Do you read a lot?"

"It depends on world events," he smiled. "The world events seem to repeat the past in the present times. The real difference is in the weapons. People still argue about the same things they always argued about; especially by the one who has the biggest ego? Ready to fight with weapons instead of words. If you have a better weapon you have to try them out especially if your words are weak. If successful, then a big war confirms you have the biggest ego. Concerning other reading material I have a whole library of good books on fishing from way back when bamboo, Heddon Pike lures, Cortland line to today's hot selling carbon tubes with dollar bills wrapped around them." I scanned TC's bookshelf and noticed some pretty interesting books, some I had read as a youngster. Those were the days just before chasing girls was more important than the secrets of the old-time fishing gurus:

STRIPER STRATEGIES

FISHING SOFT BAITS IN SALTWATER
FOUR FISH
THE ART OF SURF CASTING WITH LURES
THE STRIPED BASS BOOK
STRIPER HOTSPOTS
FISHING DIAMOND JIGS AND BUCKTAILS
IN PURSUIT OF GIANTS
THE MOST IMPORTANT FISH IN THE SEA
20 YEARS ON THE CAPE
ON THE RUN
STRIPER WARS
STRIPER SURF
THE COMPLETE BOOK OF STRIPED BASS FISHING
THE FISHERMAN OCEAN
BASS FROM THE BEACH TO CATCH A BASS
TROLLING FOR STRIPED BASS AND BLUE FISH
STRIPER MAN

CHAPTER

2

OLD BOOKS

There were a few books I never heard of nor read as:

STRIPED BASS FISHING, FRANK WOOLNER and HENRY
LYMAN, 1983

THE COMPLETE BOOK OF STRIPED BASS FISHING,
HENRY LYMAN, FRANK WOOLNER, 1954

SURF FISHING THE ATLANTIC COAST, ERIC B
BURNLEY, 1989

STRIPER, JOHN N. COLE, 1978

BAIT TAIL FISHING, AL REINFELDER, 1969

CAPT. HOWIE JACOBS 1952 GUIDE FOR SPORTS
FISHERMEN, 1952

FISHING AROUND NEW YORK, J. W. MULLER, 1950

STRIPED BASS, O.H.P.RODMAN, 1947

SALTWATER SPORTSMAN'S SECRETS, HENRY LYMAN,
1949 1953 MANUAL FOR THE FISHERMAN, STAN
SMITH, 1953

GUIDE FOR SPORTS FISHERMEN, FORSTER
PUBLICATIONS, NEW YORK, 1951, 1952.

While I was scanning through the library trying to decide which books to read first, the phone rang. TC answered and said he had to be gone for a few hours.

He said, "Ted, start reading. Years of surf fishing knowledge is enclosed in these books. Open them up, you have a lot of catching up to do. Take notes. Since it will be dark before I get back, make a sandwich for yourself. I have a cot folded along the wall and you can use it. I guess you will be staying awhile."

TC left in a hurry so I had time to learn from the old-time surf jockeys as Woolner, Lyman, Daignault, Karas etc. I felt like they would be sitting next to me as they told me their secrets. I found a notepad on the coffee table and started to take notes. Priceless notes. Decades of fishing experiences from the very best. If I could extract secrets, this library was worth a fortune. Years ago Rand McNally published a softcover book concerning travel throughout various cities in Europe. They would put you in a favorite city, in a great cafe, in a particular chair next to a certain window with beautiful hanging flowers and suggest you order a particular pastry with their hot Irish tea. After one hour of scanning the locals walking past the window, it was suggested you leave by the rear exit, step 10 paces to the right and find yourself at Irma's linen shop where the best buys were in the back of the shop on the left. Wow! After reading the travel excerpts through London, Paris, Rome, Madrid, Lisbon, etc. who needed to go there? I felt as though I was there, the smells, taste and environment. The very best of the cities, for $14.95. What a trip.

As I started to read books from TC's library, I started to feel the same as what Rand McNally offered. The books were varied in many ways but each one put me where I should have been with the author. I would scan pages that were similar to other pages and other books but from a particular unique view from each author. Similar but different. My notes were numerous after scanning about two thirds of the books but the notes tailed off towards the latter one third. There were many ways to explain how to do a particular thing because you express the "thing" in your own words. When broken down to its basic parts, many of the gurus used the same strategies. They explained it via the situation which led to their successful catch. The times, places and season were different but the results were constantly the same using similar methods. Knowledge will not only set you free from foolish fishing friends, it will make you a confident successful angler. Here are my notes from the old to the new.

1. GUIDE FOR SPORTS FISHERMEN, FORSTER PUBLICATIONS, NEW YORK, NEW YORK 1951 AND 1952.

The era of fiberglass rods, linen and nylon line, conventional reels. Well rounded booklet, 96 pages with the where and how to catch 23 species of fish with maps and tips. 23 marine maps from Montauk to Cape May, 65 tide tables. Local fishing spots, world record fish. Good book for beginners and a review for the experienced.

Featured a 961 1/2 pound tuna taken off of Rhode Island. The days of Ashway nylon squidding line, Horrock-Ibbotson Co., Power glass saltwater rods, Shakespeare and Sunset fishing line, South Bend mono line and rods, reels. Even split bamboo rods were available. Cortland Company moved from twine line to nylon line. Looking for a party boat to fish from, this guide showed you where. I counted 528 boats which offered, party boats, rowboats, with a half a dozen coastal cities not reporting on their fleet.

2. 1953 MANUAL FOR THE FISHERMAN, NEW YORK
    NEWS PUBLISHER, STAN SMITH, EDITOR OF
    WOODS AND WATERS, 1953

Fresh and saltwater review of most all species of fish, tide table, comment by Ted Trueblood, Alex Rogan, John Knight, H. G. Tappy, Dan Ryan, Eugene Marrant, Lee Wulff. Soft cover, interesting columns by noted fishermen and women. Maps covering where to fish for fresh and salt water fish in NJ, PA, MD, CT, Rl, MA, NH, VE and NY.

3. FISHING AROUND NEW YORK, F.WEIDNER
    PRINTING AND PUBLISHING COMPANY, 1950.

Where and how to catch 25 species of fish. Good chapter about the most common fish, big hook chart, swivel chart, sinker chart. Pamphlet dedicated to the good anglers who have passed and left the info for us. Cost $0.30

4. THE COMPLETE BOOK OF THE STRIPED BASS
    FISHING, NICHOLAS KARAS, WINCHESTER
    PRESS, 1974.

The fishing techniques and tackle from A to Z and beyond. The basics to the unique. The book you have to start with and keep handy in your library. First complete book of Striped Bass fishing by Nick. Several others to follow with added features. I call it the bible. 368 pages.

5. SALTWATER SPORTSMAN'S SECRETS, HENRY
    LYMAN, 1949

From the science of bamboo rod selection and making thereof, reels, 9 thread line, terminal accessories, this book was the Nick

Karas complete saltwater info softcover booklet of the 1949 era. Rod and materials have changed but not the basic science.

Reels, leaders, hooks and accessories. Surf casting with bait and lures. How to troll. Reading weather. Sixty three pages of good information for $0.50.

6. STRIPED BASS, O.H. RODMAN, A.S. BARNES AND COMPANY, 1947

Well rounded book about striped bass, tackle, techniques, conservation, total catch in years past (1885-1935), and fly fishing. A little bit of everything. Old stuff still works today. Quick read. Rodman gets down to the essentials. This is 1947 not the 21st century. He talks about the gear from steel rods, reels and lots about plugs. Many plug manufacturers have disappeared over the decades. Very little about fishing line. Conservation was highlighted in chapter 5 with the Chesapeake Bay as the center of striped bass production. He has a graph of the catch at Fort Pound Bay, Long Island, New York indicating the number of stripers caught in a pound net. It was 7500 fish in 1885 to about 400 in1935. The trend was heading down until 1936 when it jumped to about 15,000 fish.

7. 20 YEARS ON THE CAPE, FRANK.DAIGNAULT, MT PUBLICATIONS 1968

The greatest 20 years of striped bass fishing on Cape Cod. Frank tells how it was. The slaughter, the tricks, the family. Dollars flowed as the bass were beached-no limit just more dollars. All legal but also sad. The beach buggy was the key to success; get them in, get them to market and get back. The way it was may never happen again. Great read.

From a wild west fishing environment, to absolute restricted areas to fish, Frank's army (family) had the best of the early times. If Frank and family did not catch what they did, maybe the 1985 moratorium would have been further delayed. It was open season in those years. We did not know the impact of so many big bass taken from the spawning mass. Fish taken from 25 pounds to 50 pounds take 2 decades to replenish to this size and weight. Frank and others of a similar bent most likely had an influence on the future quantities of the bass migrating up and down the East Coast.

Enter the statisticians who had to count the biomass of the striped bass. Lots of luck. Statistics is the science of looking at a part of the whole and forecasting the status of the entire group. Be sure to include all the other knowns and unknowns influences. Tough business.

CHAPTER 3

NEW BOOKS

8. STRIPERMAN, SHERWOOD LINCOLN, SURE-BET LLC, 2012

Life of a rod and reel striped bass commercial fisherman from 1971-1985 in a small boat. The ups and downs of living life to catch and sell bass against fierce competition; the honest and dishonest. If you are looking for deep secret tips to catch bass, here it is. Stories of day to day fishing for a living. Stand tall else the competition will reduce you to their size. The good, bad and troubling days. It's on the job training every day and difficultly every day. No time to sit back if you are one man in a one man boat, looking to make a living off the striped bass. You had better learn something about fishing every time you go out, your competitors are.

Lots of interesting stories about fish, equipment, rubber suited divers with spears, weather, friends and foes and Sherwood's "bombs".

Sherwood prints in bold letters the secrets if you do not have time to read the whole book. You can only obtain these important points about "bassing" by trial and error. Hence tips are your gift from Sherwood without your trial and error efforts. Tip your cap to those who make a fair and honest living fishing. Since they, like Sherwood, put their time in, they know the answers. This book has those answers.

9.   ON THE RUN, DAVID Di BENEDETTO, PERENNIAL CURRENTS, 2003

David fished all the hotspots from Maine to North Carolina for striped bass. A face to face meeting with Dave as he described the ordeals of learning from the very best. Swimming out to meet the bass is a proven tactic even with the sharks. He tells you the time of the year and where to go. You can do the same. Very enjoyable conversations between Dave and his guides.

From Maine in early September to North Carolina in late November, Dave weaves a wonderful true story of following the bass as they head south. Hooking up with the right people with striped bass passion, makes for easy reading and great fun. You would think fishing with the best guides would guarantee total success. If you know a little about the striped bass that isn't necessarily so. Schoolies were the consistent catch, if he caught anything when traveling south.

It is not a show and tell book, it's an adventure said Dave who wanted to do this for a decade. He didn't go with a wad of dollars to spend on fancy hotels, he went as a striped bass fisherman looking for action at a reasonable effort of time and money with other passionate fishermen.

10. TROLLING FOR STRIPED BASS AND BLUEFISH, PETE BARNETT, BURFORD BOOKS, 2007

If you are a boat guy here is the basic text with lures, lines from mono, to braided, to lead core, strategies for the endgame. Especially the end-game from a boat. If you troll for bass, listed is all the equipment you need and how to use it. The bible for trolling.

The boats cover a lot of water and give more opportunities to find and catch bass and blue fish. Pete covers the boat, equipment in and on the boat. Location, location and location is the key for repeated success. Find them in one place and you'll find them there again. Better have" knot knowledge" when on the boat and how to handle the endgame boating the fish. Presentation is everything while trolling. You could waste a whole day with a poor presentation and not have to worry about the end game.

11. STRIPER STRATEGIES, D.J.MULLER, BUFORD BOOKS, 2008

DJ is a lure man, mostly but if fishing is catching then he'll go with the bait. When to fish for bass is when you have time but DJ gives you the best time. DJ fishes with the best bass masters. Strategies are basic for success in the surf and DJ and his friends tell it here.

There are a lots of ways to skin a cat and catch a striper, bait to artificials.DJ covers it all because he did all of it.

The 1st strategy is to know your equipment and what it can do for you and the next is to know how to fish your bait and each artificial lure. DJ covers all the well-known artificials of surface and subsurface plugs. To get to that out of reach sandbar try the Roberts 3 ounce Ranger and the Afterhours 2.5 Dook. DJ likes to modify his plugs. Improvement if possible. Bucktails without a rear tail are like bikes without pedals. Pork rind or Mr. Twister Tail will do.

Teasers are killers when bass feed on small stuff and ignore your plugs hence add a teaser to them. A two for one option.

Crabs and clams are the tidbits of the bass especially in early spring; may be the only food around.Doc touches all the bases. If you can't find the answer here, the question doesn't exist.

12. FISHING SOFT BAITS IN SALTWATER, PETE BARNETT, BURFORD BOOKS, 2008

Bucktails have been replaced with the ultimate lure-soft baits. They look like, swim like, even smell like and with paddle tails, could even sound like fish. No need to try to oxygenate your fresh bait, soft baits are ready to go 24/7. You have variety in shapes, color and size with or without lead heads. If you want to imitate the real thing, this is your book from A to Z. If you like to fish with colors take your pick from black to white and all colors in between. PVC plastic has found many places in the home and also in soft plastics. The epoxy may repair your wood/hard plastic plugs and superglue can do the same to soft plastics.

There are limits: lightweight for casting, may not sink well, some limited tail action, no noise, easily cut by fish, and limited splash attraction.

Unlike real bait you can put them in your pocket and find them later in good shape and ready to go. They are baits that are not bait. Bait shop close at 2 AM but your PVC store is always open, you have your package 24/7.

13. THE FISHERMAN'S OCEAN, DAVID A. ROSS PhD, STACKPOLE BOOKS, 2000

The science behind the environment for fishing, the dictionary. Don't leave home without this information in your mind and the book in your library. He tells you how the ocean, river, bays etc. work. The fish know, do you? Read and reread and understanding is a must. Tide, current, moon influences; become a knowledgeable fisherman.

How the ocean environment works. If you fish from shore to offshore, Ross explains how it works. Tides, current, waves at the shore, estuaries and oceans. A wonderful, useful and necessary read for all anglers. Get to know your surroundings above surf-line and subsurface landscape. The near shore line is a saltwater cafe.

Water temperature controls where fish will locate. Quick temperature changes can kill fish yet some fish can control their body temperature. Some species of fish in different regions may have different tolerances for temperatures.

Changes in salinity can be tolerated by striped bass and tarpon. Salt water is around 34% of dissolved salts. Coastal fish see poorly below 30 feet of water depth. No use trolling below 30 feet per the author.

For progressive waves (off shore) maximum and current flows at peak high tide and at peak low tide peak or occur 3 hours into flood tide and 3 hours into ebb tide. Slack tide occurs 6 hours after the start of the flood tide and ebb tide. Lazy fish love the slack tide. For boaters offshore the progressive waves are most prominent.

Standing wave found in bays, inlets and similar waters have maximum current 3 hours after the peak of high and ebb tide. Slack water at peak high and low tide.

Incoming weather can mix the action of progressive and standing waves so neither one is fully implemented. If by boat whitecaps appear, the wind speed would be at least 15 knots; return to port if you are in a small fishing boat.

14. STRIPER HOT-SPOTS SECOND EDITION, FRANK DAIGNAULT, THE GLOBE PEQUOT PRESS, 1996.

100 top surfing fishing locations from Maine to New Jersey. Ratings for each site, time, tide, lure, bait, season. If you don't have the time to stroll the coastline, Frank has done it for you. The gate opener, time-saver by the instructor. A million dollar give away. Get it, then read it, and keep it nearby. You can't buy this knowledge, you can only learn it by doing it. Frank's giving away the store. Don't leave home without it. Priceless. The when, where and with what. Great read to plan a trip to striper land from north to south.

15. FOUR FISH, PAUL GREENSBURG, PENGUIN BOOKS, 2010.

Salmon, sea bass, cod, tuna. It's all here. The guts of the business for the dollars in these fish. The world fishing fleet is 4x bigger than what the catch can sustain. Technology can direct the catch to max efficiency. Get your share before they go extinct. Maybe by the next moon. Inside the business. Follow the money crusted with sea salt and you will be next to the four fish. Dam the rivers where wild salmon run so you can farm raise them for $s. Sea bass, if we cannot stand them in the ocean, we can make them happier in the ponds around the world. The sea bass will like to stay home. Cod will be netted till they are no more, then find the rest, then no more. A decade later they will still not recover to normal numbers. Rebuilt from 12% to 50% is not a rebuilt; it's who can get more of the 38%. Fish farms know no boundaries. With water, food and technology farm raised fish can be a business most anywhere. If problems develop in a fish farm, man can probably resolve it. Yet such farms may be a negative effect on the species because of the exchange of repeated DNA in a small population.

Can the sea feed the world? Pond fish may be an answer?

CHAPTER 4

TWO BECOME ONE

TC came back to this estate to pick up some pictures before heading out again. Before he took off he told me some of his personal life. Something generally unknown in his family's history.

"One day while fishing some 30 years ago I was attracted to a woman surf caster who handled her 10 foot rod like an experienced and well-tuned expert. About 5 foot 10 she was also a beauty and intelligent. With red hair and blue eyes she was easy to watch casting away with the surf rod. She was easy to talk to especially about our common interest in the striped bass. An hour of surf casting led to an hour at dinner. It was a charming time for both of us. We plan to fish together in a month or so.

Katie lived alone just off the beach. Daily work took her to New York City by train or to the airport for various parts of the world. I mentioned my name and she recognized it since I had a fishing column in the local paper and was on the local radio station. Her business had something to do with industry and the meaning of words. Whatever she said it was okay by me. A few weeks later I read in the regional newspaper that a woman caught a 60 pound striped bass in the surf. They left her name out, but the picture looked like her and the place she caught the bass was one of the places I had mentioned to her. I continued to fish the local beaches as well as others in my travels. A few weeks later I met Katie at the old beach about the same time. We had a heck of a time talking about her big bass. It was caught at Montauk, the home of big bass. It wasn't long before we celebrated a great dinner, drinks and the roaring laughter, mostly by me. It was past midnight after I left heading to my next scheduled start. It was a magical night with a lovely woman. The striped bass brought us together. This was 30 years ago. That was the last time I saw her. I frequented the same beach for a while looking for her but to no avail. I guess she didn't want to go any further with the relationship. I respected her wishes and did not pursue it any further. Beside my wife would have had something to say about it. So that was it till the phone call. It was from Kate. I'll finish the story when I get back."

As I continued taking my notes, TC called and said he was staying overnight. He said to make myself at home and he would see me tomorrow. The fridge was good with snack food, food to be cooked, food that was already cooked and beer to be drunk. Okay by me as I continue to uncover the secrets of surf casting from the past gurus that shuffled along the sand and the novices who followed in the footsteps of these ghosts. My mind wondered what secrets TC had in his past. Must be something important like family matters but I didn't think he had a family. They didn't have kids hence that must be a close family friend.

I continued with my reading and taking notes.

16. STRIPER SURF, FRANK DAIGNAULT, THE GLOBE PEQUOT PRESS, 1992

Finding stripers day/night, surf gear, bait/lures and secrets. His third book about bass, all books of on the job training. This reads like Frank was sitting down with you telling and showing you his magic. Easy to read over and over. If you are a surf jockey, you need all of Frank's books in your library.

The inside door is opened by Frank. Inlets, nights, birds, oil slicks, bridges and shadows, daybreak and twilight, compulsive urges in the suds at 6 AM. It all can be like a drug.

Gear, rods, reels, line. For the perfectionist. The details. Eels, the king of baits. For everything else, the small details that makes the difference between Frank and you. Get to know Frank.

17. BAIT TAIL FISHING, AL REINFELDER, A.S. BARNES AND COMPANY, INC. 1969

The beginning of soft bait lures. Looks like a bucktail with a soft skirt or a small eel. Details on how to fish the Bait Tail in surf, bridge, bay, river etc. Will catch all kinds of fish. It will be close to 50 years before the chemistry is known for today's soft baits. In those days the Bait Tail was developed over 5 years. It's not a buck tail, it's a jig, a Bait Tail jig. Good review of various jigs and their uses.   164 pages

18. BASS FROM THE BEACH, VOL II, TIM COLEMAN, EDITOR GENE BOURQUE, 2008'

Very personal information from one of the best writers and fishermen along the East Coast. Lots of info, photos, places, things and more. Bass love the night hence I'm a night man. The innards of the fisherman and his soul.   140 pages

19. TO CATCH A BASS, TIM COLEMAN, MT PUBLICATIONS, 1997

If you cannot read, most everything about fishing for striped bass is in pictures. Read the pictures.

See how to use bait and lures from surf and boat and places. Tim recently died doing his favorite thing, bass fishing but he left a lot of himself in his books.

This is one of them.

From Deal jetty at Asbury Park, New Jersey to the elbow off Montauk Point, New York to Ipswich. MA. Tim was there.

Mostly bass fishing done from a boat using eels to umbrella rigs and all in between. Tim hasn't missed anything concerning fishing for bass in a boat.

Lots of pictures to illustrate how to do it right. Do you know 3 way eeling? Bunker and bucktails? What does a good Center Console include?

20. STRIPED BASS FISHING, NICK KARAS, THE LYONS PRESS, 2000

Another complete book by Nick, including who caught the big bass and where. By state, migration pattern, baits, lures, rod, reel, and line. The bible. List who caught 60 plus pound bass. Nick works from his boat but also includes the surf jockey, rocks, piers and bridges. Big bass are midnight cowboys. He also tells you how to cook the bass. The complete book from A to Z.

Nick does his charters from his boat under Saxatilis Charters out of Orient Point, New York.

21. STRIPER, A STORY OF FISH AND MAN, JOHN N. COLE, ATLANTIC MONTHLY PRESS BOOK, LITTLE BROWN AND COMPANY, 1978

John is a Maine man. There is no index in the book. The book is almost a novel with a touch of philosophy. For a time he made a living fishing for stripers. Seine net fishing can be profitable but it's a lot of hard work as you work from the beach. John made a living by planting one stake in the sand, rowed out beyond the surf dropping the seine nets and rowing back to the beach with the trapped bass. Ten thousand pounds of bass per net was not uncommon. Strife between the seine netters and the surfcasters was common since they were fishing for the same fish, in the same surf, at the same time. He knows the territory, listen to him. Only man can save creatures and so it is with the bass. Chapters full of wisdom and strife.

269 pages

22. FISHING DIAMOND JIGS AND BUCKTAILS, TOM MIGDALSKI, BURFORD BOOKS, 2008

East Coast, West Coast the jig and the bucktail cannot be beat. Why does the Navy survival kit contain bucktail jigs? He tells about the size, shape, weight, how and when to use them for all kinds of fish. Discusses the new kinds of jigs. How to land the fish and photo it. Jigs and bucktails were used before you were ever thinking of fishing.

Tom's a boat man. The boatman says diamond jigs and bucktails could catch over 90% of the fish you are after.

Diamond jigs range from 1/4 ounce to 32 ounces. Their silver sides represent herring, menhaden, sand eels, anchovies, shad, mullet and butterfish. Go with single ring rear hook or a stinger hook up front.

Tom talks about catching bluefish, striped bass, weak fish, false albacore, mackerel, school tuna, cod, haddock, pollock, black sea bass, rockfish, halibut, salmon, using vertical jigging diamond jigs and bucktails.

If you need details on rigging for fish while on a boat, Tom knows the "how"; this book is for you. Rigging for mackerel to tuna is quite different.

23. THE STRIPED BASS BOOK, MILT ROSKO, BURFORD BOOKS, 2002

Milt has written a specific book for each of the popular game fish. Now here is his bass book. From surf, jetty, rocks, boat, fly rod. Where to find them. Here comes it all. The book gives a unique view of the striped bass from experiences of many years chasing and finding them in surf, jetty, rocks, bridge, and docks. He also has recipes for the skillet. There are very few secrets but always different ways of looking at the same thing. So here is Milt's view.

East Coast, West Coast, South Coast, Milt has fished each of them. He has bits and pieces from each coast in this book. He's a jetty jock because the bass are there. Bait fishing is only good if you locate your spots at low tide. Fishing docks and bridges offer new opportunities even with a fly rod. Chumming, trolling, boat fishing, jigging etc. Lots of bits and pieces for striped bass fishing. A little of everything for every fisherman.   226 pages

24. THE ART OF SURF CASTING WITH LURES, ZENO HROMIN, by ZENO HROMIN, 2008

If you are a surfcaster don't leave home without reading it. In fact read it before you go and take it with you. Imitation, imitation the key to success. Match the hatch run in the spring to the fall for the best results. Bunker chunks in the early spring, when they are not around, brings a low probability of success. Mullet, herring, spearing in the springtime are better bets because they are there. You can't buy his experience, only read about it and apply his methods. Learn the art as taught by Zeno.

The art consist of using darters, needlefish, popping plugs, metal lip swimmers, plastic swimmers, bucktails, soft plastics, tins, and teasers.

The how. casting distance means nothing, location is everything. Perseverance and determination are the spirit of a surf caster using the proper lure for the right situation. Knowledge puts you at the right time and place. A flimsy, wooden popsicle stick will catch bass if you know the location, time/tide and art of surf casting with lures.

Darters: Stan Gibbs developed a series of them. Difficult to make correctly; small manufacturing errors make poor floating debris. Gibbs and Super Strike are good. If they don't zigzag, send them back. They are best used in the dark. Use around inlets and points. The color yellow is my only color except for white. Need current for darters to zigzag- 6 to 8 inch lengths are best.

Needlefish: A stick with hooks. Better use at night-reel slowly. About 1.5 ounces to 2.5 ounces work well at 7 inches long. They cast like bullets. The plastic ones can be loaded at the rear to 3 to 4 ounces for use in heavy weather. They sink better than the standard ones.

Popping plugs: Standard and Pencil: Best in calm waters. Vary speed of poppers to attract fish. There are sinking and floating poppers. Sinking poppers imitate dying fish trying to get to the surface. Pencil poppers like to dance on the surface especially near rocks. Fish at dawn for the best results. Good at full moon otherwise leave in the bag at night.

Metal lip swimmers: The most important lure in your bag. The lip can be altered to surface fish or for deep diving. A good white water lure in moderate to rough white water. A 6 inch to 8 inch lure works well. Not a good lure for calm waters. Best are from RM Smith, Gibbs, and Beachmaster. Subsurface swimmers are good with eel skins.

Plastic swimmers Bombers, loaded Red Fins, Yo Zuri, Rebel.

Day or night retrieve slowly and more slowly.

Bucktails and soft plastics

Bucktails the best lure ever. Good in wind, on sandy

Beaches and white water. You need a feel for the bucktail to work for you.

Work just above the sand by choosing the right weight. A twitching action is the key.

Pork rind is a must with bucktails. White color and more white is best.

Soft plastics with paddle tails represent a baitfish in motion. Their hooks may be their weak points. Heavy plastics may best be used with conventional reels.

When: inlets, before and after new moons, in current, white water, rips, wind in your face, nor'easter, sandbar, bridges etc.

Before I picked up the next book I noticed a Field and Stream Magazine on the table highlighting the 25 best surf lures ever. Jimmy Fee, an accomplished surf jockey and editor at "On the Water" magazine, was the author. Here they are in no particular order:

Creek Chub Pike, Bomber Long A, Boone Needlefish, Gibbs Pencil Popper, Cotton Cordall Red Fin, Super Strike Super 'N' Fish, Yo-Zuri Mag Darter, Andrus Jetty Caster, Atom 40, Super Strike Zig Zag, Reverse Atom, Danny Plug, Acme Kastermaster, Gibbs Casting Swimmer, Daiwa Salt Pro Minnow, Northbar Bottledarter, Super Strike Little Neck, RM Smith Swimmer,

Lunker City Slug-Go, Sebile Stick Shadd, Atom Striper Swiper, Red Gill Rascal, Storm Wildeye/Tsunami Shad, Point Jude Tins, Yo-Zuri Surface Cruiser.

25. THE MOST IMPORTANT FISH IN THE SEA, H. BRUCE FRANKLIN, ISLAND PRESS, 2007

Maybe the most important book about the food supply for many fish, especially the striped bass. Bread and water will not feed the fish but catching their food supply puts dollars in the pocket for others. This simple fish can do the most complex functions as clean up the ocean, bays and rivers. The near shore ocean environment cannot be healthy without the menhaden. A ten cent a pound fish doing a multimillion dollar job. My kind of fish.   265 pages

At the end of the book was a recent letter from The Interstate Fisheries Management Plan.

It referenced the stock of the Atlantic Menhaden. It seemed Washington, DC has directed attention to the most important food of the striped bass. In part it reads:

Executive Summary

The purpose was to update the 2010 Atlantic menhaden benchmark with the recent data from 2009 and 2011. No changes in structure or per parameterization were made to the base model run. Corrections made to data inputs were minor and are described in the body of this report. Additional sensitivity analysis and landings projections were conducted.

Abundance of menhaden has remained at similar levels as reported in the 2010 benchmark assessment. Total abundance in 2011 was estimated to be 7.84 billion fish. Generally low recruitment has

occurred since the early 1990s. The most recent estimate for 2011 (4.03 billion) is the 2nd lowest recruitment value for the entire time series, but is likely to be modified in the future as more data from the cohort are added to the analysis. Population fecundity was variable across the time series, but has declined since 1990s to 2011 terminal year estimated of 13 trillion eggs.

Fishing mortality estimates suggest a high degree of variability, but in general the reduction fishery has experienced declining fishing mortality rates since the mid-1960s, while the bait fishery has experienced increasing fishing mortality rates since the 1980s. Reduction fishing mortality rates have risen though in the last two years of assessment (2010 to 2011). The estimate fishing mortality in 2011 was 4.5.

The current overfishing definition is a fiduciary per recruit threshold of F of 15%. The current fiduciary based overfishing definition is a threshold of SSBmed (half of SSBmed). Benchmarks were calculated using all years, 1955-2011. The ratio of full F in the terminal year to the overfishing benchmark was greater than one. <u>Therefore overfishing is occurring,</u> but the stock is not overfished. However, the TC (Technical Committee) warns that there is a technical mismatch between the current overfishing and overfished reference points. The TC recommends that, given the Board has adopted an F of 15% overfishing definition, a matching overfished definition should be adopted as well. Overall, the retrospective pattern and a number of other issues just considerable doubt on the accuracy of the estimates from this update stock assessment. The TC warns that additional data analysis and modeling work are necessary to resolve these model structure and performance issues. Although the Technical Committee (TC) could not come to consensus on the utility of the terminal year point estimate of F and SSB for management advice, there was a consensus that the status determination were likely robust. In other *words the ratio of F greater than 1 (overfishing is occurring) and SSB is likely greater than 1 (the stock is not overfished), but the exact magnitude of these ratios could not be determined.*

F equals mortality   SSB equals stock of fish.
Recruitment means new fish

In January 2005 the penultimate menhaden production factory on the East Coast, Buford Fisheries Inc.in Buford, North Carolina, closed permanently. Since then, Omega Protein Inc. at Reedville, Virginia, is the sole remaining industrial process of Atlantic menhaden on the eastern seaboard. The reduction fleet at Reedville's is comprised of about 10 vessels (approximately 165-200 feet in length). Most of their fishing activity is centered in the Virginia portion of the Chesapeake Bay and Virginian's ocean waters: however, in summer the fleet ranges north to Northern New Jersey and in fall south to Cape Hatteras, North Carolina, occasionally a few smaller purse-seine vessels that fish in Chesapeake Bay for menhaden for bait, unload their catch at the Omega Protein factory when the bait demand is soft or when their catch is too small for the bait market.

A complete chronology of Atlantic menhaden landings dating back through the 19 th century, is presented in the previous benchmark stock assessment ASMFC 2010. Here recent landings are discussed beginning in 2005. Between 2005 and 2008 only the factory at Reidsville, Virginia operated. Landings ranged from 141,100 tons (2008) to 174,500 tons (2007) and averaged 155,000 tons. Reduction landings in 2008 accounted for 75% of total coast wide landings of Atlantic menhaden (bait and reduction combine) down from 80% in 2007 and 86% in 2006. During 2009 to 2011, reduction landings range from 143,000 tons to 183,100 tons and averaged 167,000 tons.

Reduction landings in 2011 accounted for 76% of total coast wide landings of Atlantic menhaden (bait and reduction combine) down from 81% in 2010 and 78% in 2009. The most severe restrictions occurred during the summers of 2008 and 2009 when vessels were often limited to daily landings not to exceed 700,000 to 800,000 standard fish approximately 213 to 243 tons or about one half the capacity of the fish holes. The factory could not handle any more menhaden.

26. STRIPED BASS FISHING, FRANK WOOLNER AND HENRY LYMAN, NICK LYONS BOOKS, 1983. FIRST ISSUE: 1954.

From the masters when we knew very little about the habits of the bass, their travels, foods, migrations. The tools needed to go get them. A classic by the very best writers. We have come a long way to understand the bass but it started with these two. Comments about each state.   192 pages

27. SURF FISHING THE ATLANTIC COAST, ERIC B. BURNLEY, STACKPOLE BOOKS, 1989

The tackle, knots, plugs, metal lures, baits, reading the beach, beach buggies, surf fishing by state in detail. Old book but fishing starts at the surf line. Eric covers it well.

The era of total access to beach had just passed. Writers such as: Burnley, Reiger, Reinfelder, Lyman and Woolner put pen to paper to tell us about the striped bass from their work and passion.

Burnley is a surf man. No radar, no boat, no fish finder, just his knowledge of sand, surf and fish. Challenge is the motivating force behind most surf fishermen. Rod and reel selection is science and art. Always look for advice in the area you fish. He breaks down what is needed in the rod, reel, line (with knots), and terminal tackle including lures are covered. He does not believe fish see color. His formula is dark color for night fishing and bright colors for daytime. Bucktails are the king of artificial baits. Waders and casting methods are covered.

Good chapter on reading the beach. Don't leave home without your beach buggy as you cover the Atlantic coast. The where and when to fish from Maine to North Carolina.   188 pages

CHAPTER 5

RELATIONSHIPS

As I finished with my notes, TC rolled up the driveway. It was well past midnight, I guess he didn't stay overnight. He looked wide-eyed and pensive at the same time, like someone hit him on the side of the head. He shuffled to the couch and plopped down. It was a few minutes before I had the nerve to ask him how he felt. No reply came for another few minutes. I tried to look busy thumbing through my notes underlining certain parts as I kept one eye focused on him. Finally I suggested we have a drink, a good, strong drink. TC meekly said it was a good idea. As we clinked glasses he started to finish the story he started before he left.

"The telephone call was from Kate. Not the one of 30 years ago, but her daughter Kate. She was headed to New York City. Her mother, my Katie, was in a serious car accident in Los Angeles, California. She lingered a few days but eventually died. Before she passed away she told her daughter about the fisherman on the local beaches loaded with striped bass knowledge, her big bass at Montauk Point and the grand celebration with the "surf fisherman, TC." The celebration night went beyond the customary congratulatory dinner, dance and good night. This Kate on the telephone was the product of that night. I never knew. That's why she probably moved on in order to keep what happened between us only between us. Kate's mother worked writing technical documents about patents. Not the patent itself but checking the meaning of words. Words must be definitive and only have one meaning. Now I knew what was meant by the meaning of words. She later got into the conservation programs. As a writer, publisher and environmentalist in California she promoted conservation via a newsletter about the striped bass in northern California's rivers and bays. She was the best friend of the striped bass and she never married. This Kate was my daughter, I could hardly believe it. Since my wife and I never had children I was dumbstruck. Happy beyond belief and I missed all those early years not knowing but knowing would have made life very complex. I offered a toast with TC on his fatherhood. We clinked glasses. The high pitched vibrations sounded like the call of church bells. Like the fading chimes of the bell, the pain of time lost was receding. Joy slowly over took and replaced it. The excitement of the moment drained both of us emotionally. After another drink and another, it was time to hit the sack. Amen.

Next morning TC said, "Ted I need some support to again meet my daughter." So I accompanied him when we met Kate for breakfast.

Although I never met TC's wife her children would have had similar features and I could see in Kate, Katie's beautiful eyes, red hair and slim shape of an athlete. She had a firm yet soft voice. Gentle and pleasant to the ear.

My daughter, Kate, married and was blessed with a son and a daughter. Everyone stayed in California. Kate was advisor, counselor, and fishing instructor to her son and daughter. Her husband worked as an aerospace engineer in Los Angeles. The family found a good home in the Southern California area and expected to stay there till retirement. Katie sent her daughter to college in Los Angeles. The daughter liked writing, the use of words, hence journalism was her career. Not the best paying job but she developed many contacts over the years in the environmental conservation arena. Many contacts from her mom and just as many by her own work. Kate took up her mom's efforts and became a spokesperson for conservation for all species. We just don't know how valuable fish and animal species are to our survival. Cancer cures or extended life strategies are already attributed to some sea life creatures. Who knows what's ahead for other flora and fauna. In her home was her mom's 60 pound striped bass and the daughter took up improving the striped bass situation in the West Coast. With about 50% of the striped bass served in restaurants coming from pond raised fish, there was no need for the commercial harvest of wild striped bass in the rivers or ocean in California. With that she pulled out a book called "Striper Wars", by Dick Russell. She said it highlighted the conflict between commercial and recreational fishermen on the beach and in the boat. Most all important battles were fought in the arena of Washington DC. Kate spoke for the bass. It is of the ecosystem that affects us all, more so for fish where their food supply swims about 0-3 miles from the shoreline. Go for it Kate.

Kate's reason to be in the area other than to see her father was that the eastern region of the coast had a striped bass tagging program. She was interested to see if such a program might be successful in the West Coast. We had a long lunch talking about "things remembered", secret things, loves lost and loves found. A feeling of apprehension came over me about my family. How things can change in an instant. TC lost his love, yet gained another. It took 30 years. I began to appreciate the love for my wife and hope it could last for 30 years and with my kids, yet to come. Kate said she had to catch the next train to New York City so our lunch ended with a promise to get together on her return trip. She would leave her notes about the tagging programs with her dad. It should be an interesting initial report.

A week later Kate said she had to get back to California. The adversaries of the environmental movement were trying to pass legislation to increase the allowable toxic materials dumped into the striped bass waterways. She would send the latest tagging program results to TC asap only with the promise he would fly to California to meet his grandchildren. Contract agreed!

CHAPTER 6

STRIPED BASS TAGGING PROGRAM

The tagging program package arrived. TC and I went through it. The tagging program for the striped bass is a coast wide study of a cooperative program coordinated by the U.S. Fish and Wildlife Services consisting of 15 states, federal and university partners. It is designated to estimate rates of expiration and mortality as well as study migration paths of striped bass along the Atlantic coast. These programs provide data necessary to manage the striped bass stock.

The central database is managed by the Maryland Fishery Resources Office. Over 500,000 striped bass have been tagged since 1985. More than 100,000 tags have been reported recaptured. Current recreational and commercial fishermen annually catch over 20 million pounds of striped bass.

Figure 1

Similar programs have begun for horseshoe. crabs and sturgeon. The federal personnel for their portion of the tagging program is funded by a $50,000 annual budget. States have their own program with their unique tags. All commercial striped bass fishermen in each state must report their catch to the government. Recreational anglers fishing for themselves are not required to report a tagged fish but are encouraged to do so. These tagged bass are probably those fish tagged by the federal employees via their boats as they survey the striped bass stock during the year or tags from the Littoral Society, Sandy Hook, New Jersey. This organization sells tags at a very modest fee. These fish would

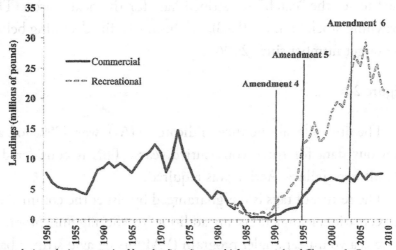

Figure 1. Annual migratory striped bass landings (in pounds) from coastal and Chesapeake Bay fisheries, 1950 – 2011. Source: pers. communication with NMFS Fisheries Statistics Division, Silver Spring, MD

have been tagged by recreational fishermen who caught under size or legal size bass and returned them to swim again. Fish caught by commercial individuals or groups are tagged when caught and sold to a licensed dealer. These tags can only be used once and are sent to the controlling federal agents. Fig. 3 sample tag from Massachusetts.

The tagging program is a check on the results of the science which attempts to assess the stock of the striped bass in the coastal areas. It is also a multi-state government and corporate program. The tags are used to confirm or dispute the statistical figures used to set the "catch" for striped bass for the next season. The spawning stock biomass (SSB), has been steadily declining below the target number since 2006.

Figure 2

The juvenile abundance indicator (JAI) was -75% of all previous data for three consecutive years. This is considered a recruitment failure. Action was required.

The return of tags is not guaranteed by either the commercial or recreational angler. As an addition to the tagging program there is a volunteer angler program (VAP) using avid striped bass fishermen. As a means of collecting additional length data, these fishermen increase the sample size but overlook lengths and weights of the sub legal or released stripers. Volunteer angler logbooks (VAL) record information about fish harvested or released during each trip for themselves and any fishing companions. Information about each trip is also recorded including time spent fishing, area fished, number of anglers and target species. At the end of the season each angler mails his or hers logbook to the Department of Marine Resources (DMR), which is copied and sent back to the angler. The National Marine Fisheries Service receive this information.

Maine

Has a VAL program with avid striped bass fisherman collecting data on lengths. About 1200 to 9200 length measurements were recorded.

Massachusetts

The VAL collect length and scale samples from striped bass captured each month, May to October for released and harvested fish. Each person is asked to collect a minimum of 5 scales from at least 10 fish per month, place the scales in a mail pouch, record the disposition of each fish released or harvested, fishing mode (boat or shore based fishing) and location. Over 2200 samples are received each year from over 100 anglers. This started in 2005. The VAL anglers adds about 100 to 1500 extra measurements to the harvested length distribution.

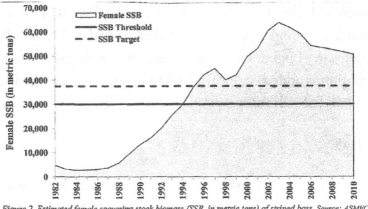

Figure 2. Estimated female spawning stock biomass (SSB, in metric tons) of striped bass. Source: ASMFC 2011 Striped Bass Stock Assessment Update.

Figure 2. Estimated female spawning stock biomass (SSB, in metric tons) of striped bass. Source: ASMFC

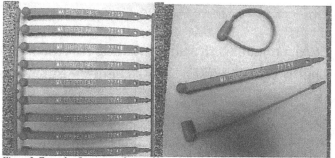

Figure 3. Example of commercial striped bass dealer tags for Massachusetts. Dealers are required to attach a tag to any striped bass shipped to a state that with tagging requirements.

Connecticut

The purpose of the Volunteer Angler Survey (VAS) is designed to collect fishing trip and catch information from marine recreational (hook and line) anglers who volunteer to record their angler activities via a logbook. The VAS anglers contribute information on striped bass, fluke, bluefish, scup, and other fish. Each VAS angler is assigned a personal code for confidentiality. The prepaid logbooks are sent via mail to the State (CT Fisheries Division). The angler gets a VAS code and updated results from the program. Logbooks are returned to the angler. The data information is added to 1000 to 3000 length measurements and sent to MRFSS/MRIP.

New York

Prior to 2011, the MRFSS/MRIP length data were not used in any fashion instead the ALS (American Littoral Society) released data to estimate length distribution of harvested fish greater than 28 inches and released fish under 28 inches. They submit information about 5000 fish per year. The ALS is a private organization which some States submit this data to MRFSS/MRIP.

New Jersey

Has 2 sources for size frequency data: a volunteer survey and the DNR Creel Survey during the spring trophy season. This trophy fish of greater than 28 inches data is reported by date, location caught and length. Data are sent to New Jersey Department of Marine Fisheries for analysis. Party boats, charter boats and recreational fishermen fill out logbooks regarding their catch. About 500 to 1500 lengths measurements are made per year.

Maryland

They have two sources for measuring size frequency. A volunteer angler survey and the DNR Creel Survey during a spring trophy season. The survey samples across sites such as docks and marinas with large angler traffic. The number of boats checked vary from 137 to 181, anglers from 182 to 461, fish from 462 to 510. Information as total length, weight, sex, spawning condition, age, scales and orthotics are collected. Other information is collected as hours fished, lines fish, boat type, anglers per boat, number of fish and fish released.

New Hampshire

About 30 to 50 volunteers per year report about each striped bass fishing trip they took in New Hampshire. Each bass is measured to the nearest inch. They report on 500 to 1700 trips per year reporting on 1000 to 7000 fish. About 95% of the fish are released.

Rhode Island

The survey of the striped bass is based on the data obtained by the American Littoral Society (ALS).

Delaware

The ALS tagged released data based for Delaware Bay, Delaware River and near-shore waters of the Atlantic Ocean are recorded.

Virginia

The Maryland data on striped bass measurement are contained in the Maryland DNR volunteer logbook survey.

North Carolina

North Carolina does not collect size or release data of striped bass.

The striped bass tagging program can only be looked at against the total striped bass program; biomass, fish harvested, fish released, fish discarded, fish tagged by federal programs, fish tagged via an ALS program, those fish tagged and never reported by recreational and commercial fishermen and natural events.

Discards:

Commercial dead discards were estimated as 625,631 and 795,675 fish from 2011 and 2012. The maximum cause for discards was by gill nets, pound nets and hook and line fishermen. Average fish age was 3 to 7 years old. Commercial bass removed by harvested and dead discards were 1.55 million and 1.63 million fish in 2011 and 2012.

Recreational harvest increased from 2.2 million pounds in 1992 to 31 million in 2006. Most of the fish were about 8 years old. Striped bass died by catch and release increased to 1.2 million fish in 1997. In 2006 dead release decreased to 460,000. Fish age averaged 2-6 years.

Figure B6.5 Comparison of commercial harvest of striped bass 1982-2012 by age (57ᵗʰ SAW Assessment Report)

Figure B6.13 Total removals of striped bass partitioned into commercial and recreational contribution 1982 to 2012

Figure B6.4 Age structure of commercial harvest in 2011 and 2012 by State

Figure B6.8 Estimate of total and dead commercial discords of striped bass by gear and areas.

Having looked at the broad expanse of data from harvested, released discarded bass in

Table B6.5. Time series of coast wide commercial harvest numbers-at-age, 1982-2012.

Year	1	2	3	4	5	6	7	8	9	10	11	12	13	14	15+	Total
1982	0	45,129	200,221	117,158	22,927	5,035	3,328	2,861	1,871	4,407	5,837	7,639	2,509	2,810	6,898	428,630
1983	0	54,348	120,639	120,999	38,278	7,416	1,954	677	607	1,690	1,314	2,375	2,656	1,856	2,733	357,541
1984	0	478,268	270,140	55,598	30,580	21,688	6,441	1,744	1,020	771	146	279	1,096	1,042	2,058	870,871
1985	0	53,699	45,492	7,545	9,448	19,248	21,569	6,581	3,692	1,514	466	607	493	894	3,373	174,621
1986	639	6,020	3,207	180	703	1,425	1,199	546	182	105	220	288	963	2,004		17,681
1987	0	0	3,087	4,265	1,618	252	1,104	1,075	448	233	95	273	302	235	565	13,552
1988	0	0	2,086	3,961	15,491	6,469	2,803	539	541	218	266	108	250	41	537	33,310
1989	0	0	0	0	0	139	1,111	959	1,007	631	475	164	343	444	2,129	7,402
1990	0	650	12,551	48,024	29,596	15,122	3,111	2,357	1,147	519	272	130	428	322	1,407	115,636
1991	0	2,082	22,430	44,723	41,048	21,614	8,546	4,412	4,816	1,163	269	125	80	553	1,937	153,798
1992	0	640	32,277	58,009	46,661	41,581	22,186	11,514	8,746	6,314	1,062	464	169	346	745	230,714
1993	0	1,848	21,073	93,868	87,447	42,112	32,485	13,829	8,396	6,420	3,955	763	184	76	404	312,860
1994	0	1,179	22,873	71,614	101,512	48,269	28,530	14,886	8,902	5,323	2,513	1,250	198	68	326	307,443
1995	0	6,726	35,190	114,519	134,709	98,471	38,918	34,191	37,324	21,827	8,364	3,166	997	363	149	534,914
1996	0	557	50,102	127,825	179,031	161,361	120,693	51,995	29,907	18,864	11,663	9,674	2,264	1,134	1,449	766,518
1997	0	1,843	37,754	342,867	213,454	206,836	102,034	76,149	54,989	30,373	17,813	13,813	4,873	3,125	2,688	1,108,612
1998	0	6,124	54,375	267,791	411,067	184,209	94,726	75,915	63,592	31,809	19,948	12,110	5,149	2,574	3,700	1,233,089
1999	0	7,591	94,342	211,645	264,460	221,773	92,992	66,837	63,357	35,916	20,939	14,180	4,611	2,549	2,621	1,103,812
2000	0	244	51,876	203,457	284,772	194,336	121,949	72,841	51,768	37,496	19,263	11,391	4,041	1,850	2,430	1,057,712
2001	0	165	86,190	189,602	241,867	140,555	89,963	95,580	34,026	31,547	22,172	12,853	5,027	2,582	692	952,820
2002	0	184	39,914	133,965	130,689	107,219	68,875	45,032	56,146	28,715	20,386	12,252	7,430	3,341	3,942	658,091
2003	0	3,932	59,027	156,836	171,626	132,005	96,662	76,612	70,049	59,722	20,916	15,944	6,647	2,366	2,472	874,817
2004	1,221	18,069	83,780	173,546	123,717	102,815	94,480	97,849	73,246	57,207	43,534	22,876	13,844	3,906	3,068	913,150
2005	0	145	43,488	239,748	252,020	102,076	57,072	56,939	75,306	50,440	41,629	25,937	19,435	4,598	4,738	973,572
2006	0	81	90,820	192,639	335,889	150,133	48,304	43,705	46,313	61,550	39,664	23,017	13,656	5,447	3,448	1,054,664
2007	0	0	4,711	305,597	207,826	190,053	78,099	51,494	64,579	51,397	32,964	20,498	9,282	3,006	3,853	1,023,358
2008	0	0	12,506	233,419	311,903	125,702	92,605	60,928	42,177	41,351	35,246	29,726	15,626	5,848	3,920	1,010,955
2009	0	69	19,745	190,560	356,448	191,280	68,995	69,342	41,636	31,813	27,531	18,630	16,438	6,490	4,534	1,043,512
2010	0	7,178	46,448	219,450	247,340	177,935	133,809	58,962	45,183	30,091	21,540	17,394	14,386	5,165	6,055	1,030,938
2011	0	788	49,592	127,860	199,887	198,523	118,074	93,069	45,488	42,628	15,586	12,507	10,349	9,153	7,987	931,490
2012	0	8,527	58,276	92,963	238,589	144,744	100,834	60,065	51,612	23,769	25,169	14,187	7,910	6,485	5,690	838,820

2012 data are preliminary.

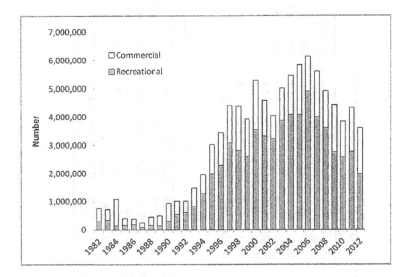

Figure B6.13 Total of striped bass partitioned into commercial and recreational contributions, 1982-2012.

Table B6.4. Age structure of commercial harvest in 2011 and 2012 by state.

2011

State								Age									Total
	1	2	3	4	5	6	7	8	9	10	11	12	13	14	15	
MA	0	0	0	35	132	562	4,933	11,321	11,953	11,888	4,367	5,148	4,550	4,927	3,493	63,309
RI	0	0	0	92	544	1,569	2,673	2,752	1,739	1,462	696	756	816	795	450	14,344
NY	0	0	0	5,254	3,280	17,193	22,244	27,449	5,398	3,918	1,306	980	327	0	0	87,349
DE	0	0	0	0	541	1,759	3,937	4,503	5,142	3,063	1,205	227	43	18	79	20,517
MD	0	0	42,782	80,375	144,116	137,283	59,336	16,680	6,445	2,212	733	422	307	175	104	490,969
PRFC	0	0	0	25,777	37,591	19,870	4,833	2,148	2,685	2,685	0	537	0	0	0	96,126
VA	0	788	6,810	16,328	13,682	19,364	18,891	25,435	10,178	15,325	6,680	4,007	3,477	3,237	3,861	148,063
NC	0	0	0	0	0	923	1,227	2,781	1,949	2,075	598	431	830	0	0	10,814
																931,490

2012

State								Age									Total
	1	2	3	4	5	6	7	8	9	10	11	12	13	14	15	
MA	0	0	0	37	138	1,308	5,582	16,616	13,353	7,676	5,671	7,015	3,089	3,359	2,550	66,394
RI	0	0	12	399	1,102	2,105	2,574	2,520	1,922	999	709	833	542	705	530	14,953
NY	0	0	0	7,418	4,175	13,431	15,208	18,732	3,846	2,291	750	600	175	0	0	66,626
DE	0	0	0	0	0	1,082	2,820	3,813	3,511	2,438	1,417	349	205	103	0	15,738
MD	0	6,959	49,218	66,050	181,941	98,053	53,022	7,075	8,175	839	664	256	0	11	33	472,331
PRFC	0	958	6,125	11,892	38,342	19,856	10,991	1,098	1,261	34	50	10	0	0	0	90,616
VA	0	610	2,920	7,167	11,809	7,170	9,645	10,497	20,464	10,467	16,915	5,252	3,952	2,410	2,562	111,839
NC	0	0	0	0	0	0	0	15	154	46	62	15	15	0	15	323
																838,820

2012 data are preliminary.

Table B6.8 Estimate of total and dead commercial discards of striped bass by gear and area.

2011

Total Discards

Area	Anchor Gillnet	Drift Gillnet	Hook & Line	Other	Pound Net	Trawl	Total
Coast	17,336	8,668	842,703	14,336	34,672	17,336	338,050
Ches Bay	895,838	398,150	597,226	0	995,376	99,538	2,986,128
Del Bay	78,097	39,048	39,048	0	0	0	156,194
							3,480,372

Release Mortality Rate

Anchor Gillnet	Drift Gillnet	Hook & Line	Other	Pound Net	Trawl
0.4275	0.08	0.09	0.2	0.05	0.35

Dead Discards

Area	Anchor Gillnet	Drift Gillnet	Hook & Line	Other	Pound Net	Trawl	Total
Coast	7,411	693	21,843	3,467	1,734	6,068	41,216
Ches Bay	382,971	31,852	53,750	0	49,769	34,838	553,180
Del Bay	33,386	3,124	3,514	0	0	0	40,025
							634,421

2012

Total Discards

Area	Anchor Gillnet	Drift Gillnet	Hook & Line	Other	Pound Net	Trawl	Total
Coast	0	18,221	318,867	36,442	18,221		391,751
Ches Bay	1,064,958	456,410	1,977,779	152,137	304,274	152,137	4,107,694
Del Bay	22,886	11,443	11,443				45,772
							4,545,218

Release Mortality Rate

Anchor Gillnet	Drift Gillnet	Hook & Line	Other	Pound Net	Trawl
0.4275	0.08	0.09	0.2	0.05	0.35

Dead Discards

Area	Anchor Gillnet	Drift Gillnet	Hook & Line	Other	Pound Net	Trawl	Total
Coast	0	1,458	28,698	7,288	911	0	38,355
Ches Bay	455,269	36,513	178,000	30,427	15,214	53,248	768,671
Del Bay	9,784	915	1,030	0	0	0	11,729
							818,756

the millions, the tag program from the commercial part of the business can be expected to be better followed than the recreational portion. Biologists at the federal level have tagged about 507,197 bass with return tags of 91,440. It is estimated there are about 22 to 200 million striped bass swimming the oceans, bays and rivers. The federal government biologists tag only a few thousand bass per year.

Eight tagging programs have participated in the USFWS Atlantic coast wide striped bass tagging programs for 18 years. The bass, highly migratory species, has two types of tagging programs: producer area programs and coastal area programs. Most programs tagged the better of: equal to or greater than 18 inches total length.

Producer area tech programs operated during spring spawning in the spawning area using pound, gill, seine nets and electroshock.

The producer areas are:

1. Hudson River fish tagged in May.
2. Delaware and Pennsylvania fish tagged in the Delaware River in April and May.
3. Maryland fish tagged in the Potomac River and upper Chesapeake Bay in April and May.
4. Virginia fish tagged in the Rappahannock River during April and May.

The coastal program is from a mixed stock during fall, winter or early spring. Capture is by hook and line, seine, gill nets and otter trawl.

1. Massachusetts fish tagged in the fall
2. New York via Ocean Haul seine survey in the fall.
3. New Jersey Delaware Bay fished tagged in March and April.
4. North Carolina fish tagged in January

Data taken the day of tagging:

1. Tag number
2. Total length
3. Sex
4. Release date
5. Location
6. Gear
7. Other data.

Data taken upon recapture directly from fishermen.

1. Tag number
2. Total length
3. Disposition
4. Recapture date
5. Gear
6. Location

Such data was used to develop statistics of the striped bass as:

1. Length frequency distribution from release to capture
2. Age frequency distribution based on fish tagged and captured
3. Annual exportation rates of the striped bass

Tag returns are small when you consider there were probably only 5 million bass swimming in 1982 and 56 million in 2007. Tag returns of less than 100,000 from 500,000 issued. High figures are stated for the producer area because these fish tend to stay in that area until the age of 3 or 4 or until a length of 18 inches or more. With tagging of thousands of striped bass from the same producer area it is likely you may recapture fish from previous tagging seasons. Such estimates of tag returns approach 50% but include estimates for errors and omissions.

Tags, if present, are also obtained from discarded fish. Total discards, alive and dead, in 2012 was 4,545,218 by all forms of capture gear. The dead discards were 818,756 fish. All forms of nets account for much of the dead discards while release fish by recreational anglers also contribute to the total discards.

The tagging program aside from the benefits of surveying the growth of the species also tracks the coast wide illegal harvest by both the recreational and commercial fishermen. Some data are available from specific law enforcement cases conducted by state and also among regions. The Interstate Watershed Task Force (IWFF) began investigating the illegal commercial harvest on the western shore of the Chesapeake Bay and Potomac River in 2003. They concluded numerous illegal activity occurred. Fishermen from Virginia were targeting large spawning fish in enclosed waters of the Potomac River and Maryland and oversized fish were taken during the spawning season and sold illegally. Wholesale dealers were complicit via false record keeping, false check- in and buying untagged fish. It was determined over 1 million pounds of illegal striped bass were taken. Nineteen (19) individuals and three corporations (3) spent a total of 140 months in prison and forty one (41) in home detentions as well as fines of $1,628,352.

Table B6.11. Time series of commercial discards 1982 to 2012. Recommendations were made:

1. Uniform commercial tagging system for all states.
2. By year, style, color, inscription.

Year	Age															Total
	1	2	3	4	5	6	7	8	9	10	11	12	13	14	15+	
1982	0	31,645	3,644	11,456	5,623	1,291	2,397	1,014	369	92	85	0	0	7	0	57,624
1983	0	24,067	1,453	2,878	7,761	2,311	610	610	262	174	0	0	0	0	0	40,127
1984	0	33,575	1,611	5,812	9,734	11,272	2,815	117	586	66	0	52	0	0	0	65,639
1985	0	7,728	30,472	5,939	10,891	3,395	2,742	1,045	261	131	131	0	0	0	0	62,734
1986	0	5,841	20,758	100,067	27,989	13,315	4,295	1,415	346	0	0	0	0	0	0	174,024
1987	0	4,206	14,382	28,597	51,389	16,940	6,520	1,319	1,011	395	111	86	111	0	0	125,066
1988	0	6,142	22,593	36,616	70,959	71,694	23,232	9,116	3,110	1,653	218	195	24	0	0	245,552
1989	0	13,854	50,240	49,029	83,396	82,757	33,479	15,502	6,342	705	1,409	1,409	663	41	0	338,827
1990	0	14,526	68,713	80,935	111,888	115,702	71,600	36,256	5,948	1,539	1,401	1,503	0	0	0	510,011
1991	79	12,632	37,009	64,210	77,335	56,894	36,912	24,857	6,610	4,071	6,542	16	0	0	0	327,167
1992	117	3,698	34,218	36,746	44,412	34,688	14,798	11,179	3,398	2,356	991	0	0	0	0	186,601
1993	0	7,449	50,160	79,011	95,116	63,487	20,941	15,351	9,270	4,606	1,651	536	260	0	0	347,839
1994	0	31,770	47,169	45,081	88,122	84,570	39,229	12,524	6,223	3,674	712	415	30	0	0	359,518
1995	0	72,822	75,520	53,551	94,158	121,592	61,447	19,083	7,569	4,269	2,290	2,346	807	0	0	515,454
1996	0	27,133	114,085	76,336	61,884	58,787	30,835	14,916	6,148	3,989	159	502	50	0	0	394,824
1997	476	7,108	64,352	61,871	30,602	20,951	14,002	6,592	1,963	4,309	2,658	801	1,060	0	0	216,745
1998	0	13,233	53,889	98,510	83,288	29,197	12,970	12,591	7,860	4,372	3,891	2,419	3,311	124	367	326,032
1999	984	58,076	49,894	43,744	55,740	14,477	5,213	3,704	1,980	1,304	648	612	240	3	0	236,619
2000	196	178,457	189,933	157,291	62,699	33,918	26,938	7,831	4,111	3,876	801	863	41	17	25	666,997
2001	0	2,638	58,079	77,958	88,808	29,410	18,877	11,613	9,664	6,371	4,778	1,957	737	10	0	310,900
2002	1,700	20,888	42,641	21,409	28,791	23,720	12,381	6,854	5,645	2,255	1,522	149	173	33	43	168,201
2003	1,512	6,227	28,061	54,464	56,728	19,866	30,850	18,633	16,410	13,572	8,164	3,207	2,894	165	1,222	261,974
2004	2,943	52,810	80,275	75,711	61,636	47,285	50,715	40,057	23,187	9,747	10,346	2,350	430	892	12	458,398
2005	432	11,456	103,594	244,697	168,622	68,032	53,795	43,376	43,305	22,961	16,102	8,439	5,216	2,008	1,463	793,498
2006	0	544	25,559	28,683	36,026	26,447	14,217	15,729	12,170	12,792	7,159	4,352	5,186	0	0	188,864
2007	288	6,276	17,910	87,979	95,757	137,620	76,994	47,593	42,024	30,344	22,250	19,923	11,803	0	0	596,763
2008	0	97	2,789	43,823	70,088	56,841	43,496	21,224	13,575	12,969	12,576	14,221	10,976	0	0	302,676
2009	0	1,645	80,587	166,064	122,265	89,464	29,830	37,602	20,328	15,330	15,678	7,649	18,236	0	0	605,677
2010	0	1,335	16,052	75,408	63,492	45,601	19,217	9,339	6,464	4,065	3,111	1,785	6,007	0	0	251,875
2011	0	3,730	58,844	105,937	125,685	80,024	56,973	56,764	41,100	34,826	16,301	12,257	9,888	9,498	13,805	625,631
2012	0	8,060	45,149	114,698	194,613	138,085	115,906	51,499	42,775	18,346	22,095	17,023	2,870	10,340	14,217	795,675

2012 data are preliminary.

Table B6.11. Time series of commercial discards-at-age from 1982-2012.

3. Tags valid for only one year
4. Be tag proof
5. Accounting for all tags used and unused with penalties if not adhered to by individuals and corporations.

Commercial striped bass fisheries occurred in Massachusetts, Rhode Island, New York, Delaware, Maryland, the Potomac River fisheries, Virginia and North Carolina. These states have many and varied aspects to how they run their programs as: days to fish, size of fish, time of day to fish, amount of fish to possess, etc.

Massachusetts did not have a commercial tagging program until recently in fact, they have been granted time to develop one. Their quota of over 1 million pounds of harvested striped bass for the commercial market left a lot of loopholes without having a tagging program i.e.; the minimum size at 34 inches and no more than 30 bass per day could be exploited. New York with nearly the same quota in pounds had a striper tagging program with full time and part time commercial fishermen. A commercial food license is also required. The Chesapeake Bay has its own tagging program with a quota of 1,430, 361 pounds and 184,853 for the ocean or coastal region. Tagging strips are different for each region. The Albemarle Sound/Roanoke River stock differs since it contributes minimally to coastal migratory fish. Its residence stock is also smaller. Only older fish show up and are from the federal program. The quota of around 500,000 pounds is evenly divided between commercial and recreational fishermen. To get a realistic figures about the tagging program between states quota and tags issued are:

Mass.	R.Island	New York	Delaware	Maryland	PRFC	Virginia	N. Carolina
Qouta: lbs							
> 1M	>200K	>800K	>200K	<2M	<700K	>1.6M	<500K
Tagged							
40K	0	25K	90K	30K	1.4M	107K	248K

>= greater than
<=less than
M= million
K=thousand

With no tags issued by Massachusetts, it indicated an opportunity to catch, not report, sell to other than licensed dealers or sell to another state. There are about 4000 commercial licenses sold in Massachusetts but very few report catching striped bass. No other state has so many commercial striped bass fishermen. The total reported catch for U.S. commercial striped bass fishermen is an average of 2.95 million pounds per year.

Massachusetts and New York account for about 60% of the catch. The quota for other States is approximately 7 million pounds for 2012. Obviously the commercial fishermen cannot catch the quota since the reported figure of 2.95 (average) million is nearly 4 million pounds shy of the maximum poundage allowed. If you add another 1 million pounds of illegal fish caught from the Chesapeake Bay area alone, you get to a figure of about 4 million pounds. It is not clear what level of illegal striped bass were caught and sold in other States. These figures are a background of the over 20 million pounds caught by the recreational fishermen. The sales of legally caught striped bass are readily followed in the commercial fishermen market but it does not exclude recreational fishermen doing the same thing. The recreational striped bass angler averages close to 20 million pounds per year with Massachusetts, New York and New Jersey (illegal to sell striped bass in N.J.) comprising 70% of the catch. The catch is equally divided. The recreational fishermen released 19.6 million fish in 2006 since then the number of fish released alive has decreased by 75% to a low of only 4.8 million fish in 2010. Reason for the decline may be attributed to less fish in the near-shore waters and/ or anglers' behavior due to economic conditions.

There is a lot of science in estimating striped bass biomass (SSB). It is similar in sampling the U.S. population when estimating the outcome of important events. You can't speak to 300 million people but a homogeneous sample of the population can statistically suggest the winner. By sampling various rivers of spawning bass each spring, the data from the catch of the latest season plus illegal catch, can give a reasonable estimate of the striped bass biomass. Approximately, very approximately, less than 1% to 5% of the biomass is allowed to be caught, loss by disease, starvation, predators, mortality on release, died as part of by-catch for other fish, pollution, low oxygen water, poor egg fertilization, sudden water temperature changes kill smaller fish, farm fertilization runoff, etc.

The striped bass biomass is a moving target from 18,782 metric tons in 1982 to a peak of 218,221 tons in 1999. The science is necessary in order to secure the species for the future.

Table 6 Recreational Harvest
Table 3 Commercial Harvest
Table 9 Average Weight by Age

It is in the interest of ASMFC to reduce the catch of the striped bass because of the decreased biomass. They have many options such as:

Proposed Management Scenarios

It is obvious the aim of the program is to reduce the catch by 20 to 30%. These are preliminary figures and are subject to the latest SSB figures. Marine life under natural law

Table 6. Recreational harvest (numbers) by age and year.

Year	1	2	3	4	5	6	7	8	9	10	11	12	13	14	15	Total
1982	0	5,721	35,125	81,725	24,916	10,953	16,943	11,960	8,970	5,980	4,983	5,980	997	997	997	217,257
1983	4,617	25,001	50,976	62,840	95,870	27,371	15,055	3,338	1,799	1,799	2,699	2,699	1,799	1,799	1,799	259,443
1984	2,021	22,316	24,474	15,610	16,528	15,288	8,034	2,548	0	849	849	0	849	2,548	2,548	114,463
1985	225	3,305	13,315	22,732	36,208	19,572	18,593	9,786	1,957	1,957	0	0	0	0	5,872	133,522
1986	11,002	5,426	9,354	12,136	12,339	13,473	12,285	18,427	7,020	4,387	2,632	877	877	877	3,510	114,623
1987	1,083	1,370	3,822	2,596	4,838	3,755	3,756	2,817	3,756	1,878	939	1,878	2,817	1,878	6,573	43,756
1988	1,023	8,155	5,116	5,120	6,135	11,214	10,191	12,225	9,169	3,056	3,056	3,056	2,037	3,056	4,075	86,725
1989	0	0	3,130	2,087	4,174	6,260	7,304	4,174	2,087	2,087	1,043	0	1,043	1,043	3,130	37,562
1990	627	7,933	17,317	39,534	22,703	22,980	16,657	15,810	7,680	3,009	1,797	899	1,797	1,797	2,696	163,242
1991	1,358	21,382	38,339	61,798	27,957	13,322	24,432	26,848	23,268	9,293	4,159	937	937	1,405	7,025	262,470
1992	1,881	15,923	61,295	52,925	54,507	20,325	13,805	23,488	23,613	18,849	3,854	1,943	971	2,028	4,371	300,179
1993	2,209	18,044	53,461	93,539	68,083	49,704	18,514	20,458	36,054	35,685	19,855	4,461	2,012	503	6,037	428,719
1994	2,112	43,976	138,180	95,461	91,957	47,419	29,827	23,833	34,809	29,969	13,650	8,815	855	427	3,846	565,157
1995	562	134,922	222,570	183,276	105,211	164,461	64,387	81,839	59,042	34,224	24,276	6,883	4,634	1,144	1,745	1,089,181
1996	531	129,149	257,038	214,669	109,361	116,156	137,033	80,275	58,041	27,210	18,534	19,437	5,627	1,535	512	1,175,113
1997	1,837	2,837	74,549	240,321	185,350	213,994	217,940	290,961	183,150	120,586	58,005	32,037	14,960	7,718	4,280	1,648,125
1998	0	20,368	133,541	229,441	168,884	164,613	134,977	153,529	163,905	95,099	87,690	41,837	31,341	14,855	15,983	1,457,063
1999	0	2,307	39,471	141,735	166,527	282,809	200,750	168,942	155,988	108,584	87,820	42,054	29,505	13,081	6,813	1,446,388
2000	0	503	37,950	255,084	402,268	357,123	423,409	201,142	120,257	97,670	53,095	28,375	17,434	10,132	10,671	2,025,112
2001	1,036	559	60,048	169,642	340,240	403,155	379,607	314,763	150,791	92,207	80,417	44,978	26,295	13,149	8,239	2,085,127
2002	0	1,530	33,823	141,000	266,095	405,275	334,964	249,670	237,556	107,817	86,338	46,611	33,558	12,795	16,128	1,973,171
2003	0	36,500	76,642	198,625	295,548	382,028	463,663	335,910	275,724	218,321	123,058	72,670	45,796	25,286	13,182	2,545,052
2004	427	214	94,601	207,895	211,670	268,011	301,427	435,274	331,997	265,634	210,003	103,559	54,859	39,501	25,272	2,550,745
2005	0	322	40,333	245,135	337,585	282,138	285,659	240,402	308,962	233,801	232,352	100,482	67,791	32,149	34,826	2,441,938
2006	0	8,326	112,441	209,402	377,324	335,684	245,484	289,948	249,576	341,499	248,790	158,204	107,653	41,432	66,863	2,788,125
2007	0	73	25,066	333,424	269,399	403,913	267,964	239,743	269,469	267,806	182,806	133,849	62,176	35,214	32,598	2,523,500
2008	0	246	7,036	74,691	340,359	211,594	473,211	359,388	200,562	243,217	197,085	156,271	103,591	36,841	61,936	2,465,018
2009	0	970	15,868	103,386	228,966	429,381	221,964	309,080	169,576	122,503	132,590	111,295	104,888	38,709	51,521	2,040,680
2010	0	8,973	25,576	141,402	156,926	288,769	487,683	201,524	215,001	155,490	81,649	79,440	58,948	37,431	47,595	1,985,415
2011	0	8,101	33,913	89,551	176,603	330,321	360,950	542,248	186,305	174,692	84,264	63,411	60,207	63,773	55,859	2,230,256
2012	880	5,750	37,455	51,034	138,448	166,043	230,082	267,495	275,475	91,442	91,694	60,174	36,369	35,751	57,521	1,545,614

Year	Age															Total
	1	2	3	4	5	6	7	8	9	10	11	12	13	14	15+	
1982	0	45,129	200,221	117,158	22,927	5,035	3,323	2,861	1,871	4,407	5,837	7,639	2,509	2,810	6,898	428,630
1983	0	54,348	120,639	120,999	38,278	7,416	1,954	677	607	1,690	1,314	2,375	2,656	1,856	2,733	357,541
1984	0	478,263	270,140	55,598	30,580	21,688	6,441	1,744	1,020	771	146	279	1,096	1,042	2,058	870,871
1985	0	53,699	45,492	7,545	9,448	19,248	21,569	6,581	3,692	1,514	466	607	493	894	3,373	174,621
1986	0	639	6,020	3,207	180	703	1,425	1,199	546	182	105	220	288	963	2,004	17,681
1987	0	0	3,087	4,265	1,618	252	1,104	1,075	448	233	95	273	302	235	565	13,552
1988	0	0	2,085	3,961	15,491	6,469	2,803	539	541	218	266	108	250	41	537	33,310
1989	0	0	0	0	0	139	1,111	959	1,007	631	475	164	343	444	2,129	7,402
1990	0	650	12,551	48,024	29,596	15,122	3,111	2,357	1,147	519	272	130	428	322	1,407	115,636
1991	0	2,082	22,430	44,723	41,048	21,614	8,546	4,412	4,816	1,163	269	125	80	553	1,937	153,798
1992	0	640	32,277	58,009	46,661	41,581	22,186	11,514	8,746	6,314	1,062	464	169	346	745	230,714
1993	0	1,848	21,073	93,888	87,447	42,112	32,485	13,829	8,396	6,420	3,955	763	184	76	404	312,860
1994	0	1,179	22,873	71,614	101,512	48,269	28,530	14,886	8,902	5,323	2,513	1,250	193	68	326	307,443
1995	0	6,726	35,190	124,519	134,709	98,471	38,918	34,191	37,324	21,827	8,364	3,166	997	363	149	534,914
1996	0	557	50,102	127,825	179,031	161,361	120,693	51,995	29,907	18,854	11,663	9,674	2,264	1,134	1,449	766,518
1997	0	1,843	37,754	342,887	213,454	206,836	102,034	76,149	54,989	30,373	17,813	13,813	4,873	3,125	2,688	1,108,612
1998	0	6,124	54,375	267,791	411,067	184,209	94,726	75,915	63,592	31,809	19,948	12,110	5,149	2,574	3,700	1,233,089
1999	0	7,591	94,342	211,645	264,460	221,773	92,992	66,837	63,357	35,916	20,939	14,180	4,611	2,549	2,621	1,103,812
2000	0	244	51,876	203,457	284,772	194,336	121,949	72,841	51,768	37,496	19,263	11,391	4,041	1,850	2,430	1,057,712
2001	0	165	86,190	189,602	241,867	140,555	89,963	95,580	34,026	31,547	22,172	12,853	5,027	2,582	692	952,820
2002	0	184	39,914	133,965	130,689	107,219	68,875	45,032	56,146	28,715	20,386	12,252	7,430	3,341	3,942	658,091
2003	0	3,932	59,027	156,836	171,626	132,005	96,662	76,612	70,049	59,722	20,916	15,944	6,647	2,366	2,472	874,817
2004	0	18,069	43,488	173,545	165,233	102,815	94,480	97,849	73,246	57,207	43,534	22,876	13,844	3,906	3,068	913,160
2005	1,221	145	90,820	239,748	203,508	102,076	57,072	56,939	75,306	50,440	41,629	25,937	19,435	4,558	4,738	973,572
2006	0	81	4,711	192,639	421,996	150,133	48,304	43,705	46,313	61,550	39,664	23,017	13,656	5,447	3,448	1,054,664
2007	0	0	12,506	305,597	260,030	130,053	78,099	51,494	64,579	51,397	32,964	20,498	9,282	3,006	3,853	1,023,358
2008	0	0	0	233,419	321,407	125,702	92,605	63,928	42,177	41,351	35,246	29,726	15,626	5,848	3,920	1,010,955
2009	0	0	19,745	190,560	356,448	191,280	68,995	69,342	41,636	31,813	27,531	18,630	16,438	6,490	4,534	1,043,512
2010	0	7,178	46,448	219,450	247,340	177,995	133,809	58,962	45,183	30,091	21,540	17,394	14,386	5,165	6,055	1,030,938
2011	0	788	49,592	127,860	199,887	198,523	118,074	93,069	45,488	42,628	15,586	12,507	10,349	9,153	7,987	931,490
2012	0	8,532	58,497	87,861	250,673	139,183	99,949	53,740	59,019	22,634	25,562	13,779	7,732	6,480	5,688	839,329

Table 9. Average catch weight (kilograms)-at-age by year.

Year	1	2	3	4	5	6	7	8	9	10	11	12	13+
1982	0.13	0.64	1.09	1.54	2.42	3.75	4.83	5.79	6.2	8.68	10.8	11.2	14.05
1983	0.2	0.55	0.94	1.37	2.37	3.29	3.77	5.36	6.01	8.1	9.57	10.39	11.11
1984	0.24	0.6	1.69	1.62	2.67	3.39	5.07	5.65	6.76	7.76	8.41	12.65	12.38
1985	0.06	0.61	1.07	1.66	2.19	3.59	4.91	5.46	6.77	7.45	9	10.69	13.91
1986	0.14	0.57	1.27	2.4	2.44	3.12	3.95	5.05	5.44	6.09	7.75	9.16	12.78
1987	0.2	0.77	1.41	2.11	2.5	2.91	3.61	4.74	5.52	6.49	7.77	9.78	13.15
1988	0.31	0.91	1.1	1.98	3.12	4.02	4.38	4.7	5.24	5.62	8.58	10.4	13.27
1989	0.16	0.83	1.22	2.23	3.06	4.53	5.37	6.23	6.04	8.68	8.94	9.74	13.36
1990	0.08	0.89	1.14	2.05	2.35	3.83	4.91	5.96	5.7	5.97	7.44	9.08	12.6
1991	0.21	0.92	1.29	2.17	2.62	3.17	4.81	5.64	6.46	6.24	9.45	8.3	14.22
1992	0.1	0.69	1.31	1.93	2.81	3.67	4.9	5.79	6.96	8.15	9.77	12.44	13.97
1993	0.07	0.76	1.31	1.99	2.77	3.58	4.8	6.11	7.03	8.01	9.53	10.76	14.55
1994	0.24	1.05	1.69	2.21	2.85	3.5	4.94	6.2	6.8	7.53	9.73	10.69	12.73
1995	0.28	0.7	1.35	2.18	2.77	3.65	5.38	6.16	7.27	8.86	7.57	9.73	16.66
1996	0.14	1.05	1.47	2.32	3.23	4.52	6.39	7.11	7.81	9.2	9.31	10.1	13.7
1997	0.13	0.62	1.18	2.46	2.81	3.64	4.51	5.07	6.73	9.17	9.94	10.24	14.78
1998	0.39	0.77	1.2	1.62	2.25	2.95	4.69	5.66	6.82	7.03	7.76	9.87	11.87
1999	0.62	0.9	1.11	1.44	1.91	2.51	3.36	5.03	6.56	7.85	8.69	9.76	11.98
2000	0.37	0.55	1.1	1.45	1.96	2.79	3.89	5.09	7.11	7.37	9.7	10.7	13.55
2001	0.16	0.38	1.12	1.75	2.21	3.25	4.12	5.02	6.36	7.79	8.65	8.29	10.87
2002	0.12	0.31	1.06	1.51	2.18	3.17	4.19	5.48	6.03	7.56	9.09	9.75	11.52
2003	0.1	0.6	1	1.4	2.2	3.2	4.1	5.2	6.1	7.2	8.5	9.4	11
2004	0.23	0.33	0.84	1.40	2.43	3.11	4.14	5.17	6.07	7.12	8.18	9.03	10.71
2005	0.13	0.50	1.14	1.64	2.22	3.23	4.18	5.64	6.38	7.21	8.51	10.00	12.19
2006	0.18	0.38	0.81	1.35	1.96	2.80	3.84	5.35	6.70	7.41	8.58	9.40	12.05
2007	0.10	0.46	0.94	1.30	2.10	3.07	4.31	5.32	6.89	7.84	9.39	10.12	12.77
2008	0.21	0.45	1.04	1.43	2.14	3.47	5.05	5.51	6.69	8.26	9.19	9.82	12.00
2009	0.26	0.62	1.03	1.41	1.92	3.29	4.49	5.74	6.87	7.73	8.81	9.47	12.24
2010	0.16	0.70	1.11	1.41	1.99	3.34	4.27	5.21	6.27	7.65	8.97	9.15	11.59
2011	0.20	0.52	1.04	1.55	2.00	3.08	4.10	5.13	6.41	7.54	8.20	9.98	13.08
2012	0.27	0.7	1.31	2.27	3.11	3.61	4.34	5.37	6.22	7.74	8.8	9.66	12.51

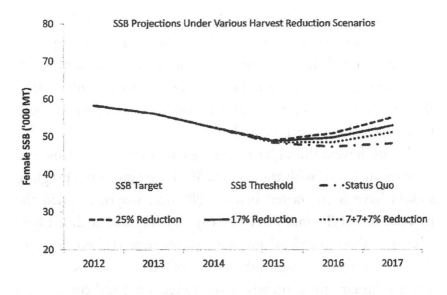

The following section outlines four management scenarios (including status quo) that are designed to reduce F to a level that is at or below its target within a one or three year timeframe. These scenarios, which are all mutually exclusive, include (A) status quo; (B) a 25% harvest reduction from 2013 levels to take place in 2015 to achieve F target in one year; (C) a 17% harvest reduction from 2013levels to take place in 2015 to achieve F target over three years; and (D) a 20% reduction from 2013levels taken incrementally through a 7% reduction in 2 A 7% reduction for three consecutive years is equivalent to an approximate 20% reduction over the three year period. For example:Inthe first year harvest (100 pounds for this example) is reduced by 7% (100 lb- 7% 931b). In the second year, harvest is reduced by another 7% (931b -7% = 86.5 lb). In the last year, harvest is reduced by a final 7% (86.5 lb - 7% = 80.4 lbs). So harvest in the last year is 80.41b and harvest in the first year was 100 lb which means the overall reduction is 19.6% or approximately 20% from the first year.

It varies in cycles and the ASMFC tries to maintain the stock while working in the natural cycle of more and less of all species. Nature has its own playbook to balance the field between species.

Man through his activities of production, produces products that interfere with the natural cycles. If we cannot totally control the products that interfere with the fishes' natural cycle, we can try to control the quantity of the catch.

We both went through the tagging data from time to time and we were surprised with the figures. We both agreed the program should have been started before 1985 and maybe avoided the moratorium of the mid-80s and early 90s. TC said he didn't hear anything about a federal program since there was no program then. He could have tagged thousands of bass over the years. This was a voluntary program where the recreational and commercial anglers could have participated for the benefit of both parties and the species. The recreational tagging program is free but the tags cost money. You purchase the tags through the American Littoral Society at www.littoralsociety.org. Some training is necessary before the bass can be tagged or more harm will be done. The government tagging program is exclusively for the marine biologist. They net and tag the bass, take length and observed their health. This fish when caught should have the tag sent to: Maryland Department of Natural Resources, Striped Bass Program, 580 Taylor Ave., B2, Annapolis, MD 21401.

If a commercial fisherman catches one of the government tagged stripers, he doesn't have to forward the tags to the appropriate agency. The commercial fishermen only uses his tags when he catches the fish and attaches his tags to the dealer who purchases the fish. There should be no commercially tagged striped bass fish in the ocean.

The tagging program had some important trends other than the ups and downs of the striped bass population. The migratory stock of the Atlantic striped bass is comprised largely of fish spawned in the Chesapeake Bay (Maryland and Virginia) and the Hudson River (New York). The Roanoke and Delaware River stock are minor contributors to the migratory stock. Mature striped bass in the Chesapeake Bay stock were born in early spring and migrate northwards in the late spring even to New England. In the winter they move south to winter grounds off the coast of North Carolina. Mature striped bass of the Hudson River origin spawn in late spring, move north then eastward in the late spring and early summer and then southwards in the autumn. Consequently a mixed stock occurs in coastal waters during the summer and winter. The growth rates of juvenile bass from the Atlantic coast indicate that growth rates are positively correlated with latitude. For other size bass there was is no such correlation. Eighty five percent of the returned and tagged bass were by anglers whether tagged by federal researchers, commercial anglers or others.

Those very small (10 em length) bass released in the northern locations (New Jersey, New York and Rhode Island) grew significantly faster than those released in southern areas (North Carolina, Maryland, Virginia). Larger bass growth rates showed little difference in northern or southern waters. Differences may result from genetics, food availability and competition.

As we talked about the impact of tagging programs, the topic to tag and release the 40 pound bass, the cows, made more sense. Tagging and releasing such a catch may give you an option to get an extra legal size bass. A few scales from such a big bass could be all one needed as evidence. It has been estimated that for every 60 pound bass caught there would be about 50, fifty pound bass caught. Female bass of that size would be a gift to the longevity of the species. Some data indicates older bass are poor reproductive fish.

TC contemplated on the outcome of juvenile bass if a world record striper would have been released. He let it slip he had been in contact with Greg Myerson, the world record holder at 88.18 pounds. I asked how this had happened. He said he wanted to congratulate Greg for catching three-60 pound bass in one year. One 60 pound bass in a lifetime is a rare event. Three is unheard of. I asked him if he would send me a picture of the world record bass. He not only did it but his story as well as a story of his three - 60 pound bass in one season. Apparently he has some knowledge of my fishing experience through the local radio station and the fishing "hotspot" news. TC went to his library and pulled out the story of the three-60 pound bass followed by the world record striped bass story.

CHAPTER 7

GREG MYERSON THREE 60+ STRIPED BASS IN ONE SEASON; AS TOLD TO THE AUTHOR.

When I was 12 years old I learned something that many people in the state of Connecticut did not realize. How awesome is it to be out on the water on Long Island Sound. What a beautiful place. There is a peacefulness I get looking back at the land and all the hustle and bustle and think man doesn't know what he is missing. Watching the leaves change color from out there is one of the most beautiful sights in the world and the place is loaded with striped bass.

When I was 12 I was invited on a boat of my father's friend to fish the Race. The Race is a hostile body of water because of Long Island Sound funnels into a narrow body of water, causing a rip. Sometimes the water is flat on the Sound side yet you can drift towards a 12 foot wall of water on the ocean side. It is always filled with fish and boats. The striped bass fishing there is some of the best in the world. Not only did we hook a lot of bass, I got hooked too.

My parents Herbert and Diane Myerson, who were both from Brooklyn, New York love to watch me fish but this was not their passion. They saw how much I loved it and helped me get my first boat, a 17 foot wooden Brockway. Old man Brockwood, a salty, old carpenter, made boats right in his yard by bending wet wood around trees and hoisted boats using an old Cadillac as an anchor, as part of a block and tackle system.

I used money made trapping muskrats, raccoon and fox to buy my motor. Muskrats brought up to $12, raccoon to $30 and more for red fox. These furs brought me a 30 hp, 1968 Evinrude. My parents told me not to go past the Bradford town dock, a short distance from where my boat was kept at Pier 66 Marina. I would take off on summer mornings and navigate to the Race and Plum Gut. If the weather was good I would fish the Gut but a lot of times it was too rough. Alternates were the Race and 6 Mile Reef which were usually much calmer. I fished for striped bass with eels and I loved it.

After 4 years at Lyman Hall High School and voted football All-American and All-State defensive end in 1985, I got many scholarship offers. I received offers from Tennessee and Syracuse but went to the University of Rhode Island to major in my true passion, striped bass fishing. When I wasn't on the field or in the class, I was fishing Narragansett and Jamestown with an old green/ white Penn 704 reel. My one and only rod was a 10 foot fiberglass surf rod with a cork handle that belonged to my great uncle. I caught some monster bass at the Beaver Tail Lighthouse in Jamestown, Rhode Island and became a good friend Greg Zeck. Greg wrote a fishing column for the Jamestown Press and had a tackle shop, Zeck Creek, held up on pilings in a salt water marsh. It was an awesome bait shop on the island. One year I watched him catch a 60 pound bass on Halloween with a surface plug like the Creek Club. That was unbelievable.

I loved to hear him talk about his fishing stories and explain the hotspots around the area. In his shop on the wall were pictures of big fish caught around Jamestown. I made the wall several times.

Big fish travel with big fish, so if you catch a huge bass there is probably another one down there. After college I got a small Westwind boat with a 70 hp Johnson and fished a lot around New Haven. I caught some nice bass at a place called Townsend Ledge. The Ledge is about 3 miles off Lighthouse Point near a reef and a pile of rocks. Bass and the blackfish hover there. A huge red buoy is easy to spot if you are shy of instruments.

I started fishing with Mr. Carlson, owner of a wood flooring store and a hard core bass fisherman. He had a muddy river running through his North Haven, Connecticut property and allowed my friend and me to fish for trout. When he saw how much his son and I loved to fish, he started to teach us the fine points of "bassing". He also took me to Montauk and the Race many times. The Race and Montauk Point are as famous as Race Point, Massachusetts, Sandy Hook, New Jersey and Cape Hatteras, North Carolina. Man I love those trips.

As soon as I had the means I bought myself a Triton 18 foot center console. Very cheap to store, run, dock and I'm able to fish almost anywhere with it. You can get awesome bass fishing within 20 minutes or less. I became a regular at Jackson Shoreline Bait and Tackle in Westbrook. Jack is a funny guy, a big, tall brute who can hold his own with anyone. His shop is next to where I dock my Triton and he will leave me all the eels I need for night fishing.

The guys in the area know how to fish. With all my striped bass fishing experience, I started to pinpoint the best places, time and tide to catch the biggest fish and mark those spots. Jack, of Jackson Shoreline, would say "Why don't you enter those tournaments, you will win". So last year I finally did. I fished hard and went especially to the places where I had the best chance to hook monster bass. For me the best time to catch a really big fish is the slack high tide, no wind, half-moon and with the biggest eels you can find. I am talking about 2 or 3 pound eels. The small bass can't eat them and the big bass can't resist them. I am talking about 50 pound plus fish. You will need a tuna rod and reel loaded with braided line because big bass don't hit hard. They are very lazy, that's why they feed when the tide is slack. They don't like to work for food, they don't like fast water and they are most always with lobsters. You have to get them in quickly or risk losing them to a lobster pot. That subtle strike is best dealt with braided line. They know quickly if something was up with the eel. They will spit it out before you even know they took it. I have caught some monsters before tournament fishing, including one fish over 70 pounds caught in 2006. I released it.

I sometimes kick myself in the ass for letting that one go but I got its picture and weight. Sometimes you have to give something back to create something good, fishing karma. My cheap spring scale settled a little over 70 pounds but how much over? That's what haunts me. Nevertheless last year was my year.

I entered the 2010 "On the Water" magazine Striper Cup. That is the premier striped bass tournament in the world. These guys do it right. Their awards ceremony on Cape Cod in October called "Striper Fest" is unbelievable. I hit all my spots at the right time and caught 3 fish in the 50s and 3 in the 60s. One fish was almost 70 pounds and won the tournament plus the title "Striper of the Year."

The combined weight of 3 biggest fish wins the tournament and the title "Angler of the Year" honors. I won both of them in 2010. It was like a dream come true. That big bass that won the tournament was a fighter. I didn't have any big eels the night before and was catching a lot of smaller bass, by smaller I mean

40 pounds, no slouch for a striper. If the 40 pounders are around so are the 50s, 60s and 70s. So the next night I came with giant eels. I remember telling Jack I wanted the biggest eels you can get. They laughed at me at the bait shop when Jack put an eel in my pocket that no one in their right mind would buy at $1.25 but maybe for Christmas dinner or a sushi restaurant. That one was the golden eel. At slack tide I dropped it right down on top of a hump in my favorite spot and felt a bump and then another. Now when you catch a lot of bass your whole life, you know when you set the hook, just what you've got. You can tell how big right away. When you set the hook and nothing moves, you have something big. My buddy Rick was in his boat drifting next to me and said "What do you have, a lobster pot?" I said. "No dude, this might be the world record." Without the heavy stick and Berkley's braided Gorilla line, I would never have landed that fish. Being slack tide he took me for a 200 yard ride in my little boat. Luckily I had my buddy, Brian with me to net the fish. Fortunately I had a good hook set and she came to the surface quickly hence avoiding the lobster pots below.

Against my better judgment and with no place to store the fish of that size, I headed to an official weigh-in station. I knew there were a lot of big fish around that night but I just couldn't take a chance of not weighing the one in front of me. I cruised under the singing bridge and didn't make it past Bill's Seafood Restaurant without everyone seeing this fish. They made me pull up to the outside bar so everyone could see it. I felt like a rock star. But that was nothing until they had me lift the fish in front of thousands of people. I took pictures with dozens of people all for just doing what I love. You can't beat that. People now, don't say, "Oh yea, he's the electrician" or they say "he's a big bass fisherman". How cool is that?

Story of the World Record striped bass by Greg Myerson; as told to the author.

I was working with Greg on his story about the three 60 +pound striped bass he caught in one season in 2010. He sent me the story via mail from his home. We both worked on it making sure he expressed the story as he wanted it.

On the morning of his world record striped bass I got a call from Greg about even a better story; a possible world record striped bass he just caught. We discussed the way to proceed with the media and the IGFA. A week later I was at his home in Connecticut to get the following story. Soon afterwards the IGFA confirmed his 81.88 pound striped bass was a line class and all tackle world record.

Big bait Big Fish Big Bass Man

Greg, good morning it is nice to be here in North Branford, Connecticut

Before we get to your story about your world record striped bass, what was your routine before going fishing that day?

My routine is about the same every day. Eat, little sleep, some work and the rest, fishing. I spend time every day figuring where to fish that night. I give my fishing buddies a call and check if they want to fish with me. I select the perfect time to be out there and then let them know what time to meet me at the dock. If some are busy I will find another. My close fishing buddies are: Matt Farina, Eddie Serrano, and Brian Bochamp. They are all good bass fishermen, all about my age and we have fished together for years. They know what work is necessary and required on a bass boat. I don't want to baby-sit anybody. Our time is too valuable.

For instance I don't want to have someone ask me "Where is the eel cache?" They also know to keep quiet while on the boat. We talk very little. The bass are not stupid and will react to man-made sounds. In fact we fish without shoes. Noise on the deck can be heard by the bass 20 to 60 feet under the boat.

I have an 18 foot center console Triton. I use it hard and it's hammered but it has been refurbished several times usually during the winter. I bought a new Evinrude motor in 2001 with the boat and it probably has 1 million hours on it. The motor has been rebuilt many times. I change props like I change socks.

I usually fish the Eastern Long Island Sound although I will go to the coastal part of Montauk. The tide from the east is cooler than the outgoing tide. Certain times of the year you should fish the incoming tide rather than the outgoing one especially at Plum Gut, the Race and many other spots. If you are trying to catch a big fish you do not want to go where the current runs fast. I look at all the data and figure out the best time and where the bass will be. The best time for me is the half-moon moving to full moon position or after the full moon and going down to another full moon phase. The moon has to be high above me at sunset, it sets up what I call the perfect time. That day you will catch big fish. The new moon phase is terrible. It's terrible on Long Island Sound because we have the phosphor iridescence in the water that makes the eels glow. It's an unusual presentation. It spooks the bass and the combination of a fast current eliminates a chance of catching big fish. Remember you do not have much time to fish if you will only fish during the perfect time. Another problem is that bluefish love to prowl the waters at this time even though the new moon is the worst fishing time for me in this area. I sometimes fish it anyhow. I never fish in the morning only at sunset because I am not an early riser. I don't think of getting up much before 9 AM and that's a good reason for me to fish in the evening.

When you are not fishing what occupies you?

I am a union electrician by trade and I try to select my jobs as often as possible. Most jobs are at the Millstone Nuclear Power Plant. The union often allows me to choose these jobs since I work there frequently. During the wintertime I will do a plant shutdown which will provide me with an excellent hourly rate. Sometimes I will go in the early fall and do the same thing and may collect a half year's salary for a month's work. I also love to hunt and hence schedule work that offers me time to hunt especially during the bow season. Bow hunting to me is just as big as striped bass fishing. In this area the white tail deer is the prime game. The water company has a tremendous amount of land and each year I get to hunt on it because they need to cull the herd. I also can hunt on the land behind my house as well as other private land of my friends. I take what deer I need for food and will give deer meat to others in need. That pond you see out there in front of my house has a great number of big trout and I feed them. It's on my land hence it is private property. It is also great for teaching my daughter about fishing.

Where is the marina you dock your boat?

I fish out of Pier 76 with my boat tied up at Bill's Seafood Marina. It is a seafood bar restaurant etc. Great place to come to after a fishing trip. I get what's running from Jack's Bait and Tackle Shop in Westbrook. All have to do is give Jack a call and he will leave me all the eels I need for the early evening fishing trip, about 2 dozen. I can run one whole tide on about 5 gallons of fuel with my 115 hp Evinrude motor: I pay for the fuel and my fishing buddies pay for the eels. I think that's fair enough. With the electronic instruments I have on board the boat, I don't ever have to look at the fishing rods. The depth finder and fishfinder let me see the fish. These are the best of Garmin's instruments and I can even distinguish a bass from a bluefish. I usually drift over reefs about 50 feet deep. The reefs usually come up about 30 feet and then drop down again. As soon as I come down the backside and nothing is there, I move to another spot and another drift. I usually let most of my fish go unless someone wants to keep one. In this State we are allowed to keep two fish per day. My Italian friends love to prepare bass and they will get one if they offer me dinner.

Before I go about fishing any evening I have all things covered like tide, wind, current, moon phase and water temperature. I try to put myself at the right spot, at the right time, in the right tide with the right bait.

The night of the world record striped bass

August 4, 2011 was the night I caught the world record striped bass. I fished that night with Matt Farina my good friend. We left the dock about 7:30PM and went directly to my best spot where I usually catch big fish. The first drift I had a good strike. The area contained a big boulder about 15 feet high off the bottom. Usually one or two big fish will be there. The "boss fish" will be there. I caught two fish on that drift, the big one and another at 58 pounds. The big one was a female and the smaller one a male. They were a pair. This was about 8 PM right about sunset when the tide was just starting to recede. The perfect time, the perfect place, the perfect fish. When I felt the fish, I knew it was a bass and I set the hook firmly. It didn't move then I laid into it. I was using a St. Croix tuna rod with a roller tip. The rod was custom built by a retired Air Force helicopter pilot that flew Marine One for three presidents of the United States. He had served several tours in Vietnam and was shot down a few times and also shot in the face. His name is Whitney Meyday. His son and I shared a room together before he passed away. I have pictures of Whitney with other presidents at Camp David.

When the fish was hooked it took off like a rocket, immediately peeling off 60 yards. I could see the line coming up to the surface of the water. I said to my buddy Matt, "He's going to porpoise;" usually big ones do this. Once they bust the surface it is difficult for them to get back down into the depths of the water. So she crashed the surface and I was amazed to see the biggest fin I ever saw. It was still light and I could see this massive fin slicing through the water creating its own wake. She was still a ways from the boat and just swimming around like cruising down the river on a Sunday afternoon. What a strong swimmer. Her broader body being always sideways prevented me from moving her towards the boat so I let her keep her distance. That went on for about 20 minutes. There was still plenty of twilight even at that distance from the boat as Matt and I froze and gazed at her. We were not prepared for all of this! Fortune shone on me that night because if the bass went deep. It was a good chance she would have fouled the line on numerous lobster pots.

The eel I use at that time probably weighed about 2 pounds. The reel was a Quantum boat reel with 50 pound braided Berkeley line. I won that reel at "On the Water" striper contest in 2010. Since then I probably receive a half dozen more.

My "fish on" boat procedures now took place. When a fish is on everyone reels up while the angler with the fish reels in. The boat is equipped with lights on both sides of the boat. When one is fighting a fish on that side of the boat, another turns on the lights on both sides. All the lights are turned on because the fish will usually swim on both sides. This helps all of us see what is going on and helps us make the right decisions. The fish now was still swimming on the surface and swimming towards the boat about 30 feet out as I frantically reeled in line. A ton of line. Then a second run. Her second run was not nearly as dramatic as the initial surge and she wasn't trying to go deep. My buddy Matt got the net and tried to net the fish at the swim platform that I had lowered. The net got stuck on the platform. I thought, "My God we are going to lose this fish right at the boat." The net was one of those gigantic ones needed for big fish. The fish got mostly into the net that was caught on the platform. Just as I reached in to grab the fish myself, the net freed itself. At that time I was just hoping the hook was stuck right knowing the hardness of the bass's mouth. The hook was a 6/0 Gamakatsu, straight up, straight down, not a C hook. I change these hooks three or four times a night because they are so sharp that it is almost impossible to notice that the tip of the hook has broken off. Unless you run your finger across it and if it doesn't bleed, the hook has lost its point. With this hook I go through the lower jaw of the eel and out its nose. My boat has a permanent stain on each side of the gunnels where we trash the head of the eels. You can call this the sacrificial altar on my boat. The eels are beaten senseless so they cannot curl themselves around the line. I said before I batter the eel, "This is hurting me more than this hurting you." A small kiss and away it goes. Nothing personal, it is strictly business, just like the scene in the movie picture "Taken." The whole battle lasted about 20 minutes. I was trying to get it in as quickly as possible but didn't want to break the line or dislodge the hook. The leader was 50 pound fluorocarbon about the length of my fishing rod. The custom tuna rod was 6 ½ feet long.

With rod in one hand, net in the other, Matt and I hauled up the fish into the boat. As we did this I received a payback for all those eels that I had bashed against the altar. With no shoes on I slipped and crashed into the gunnel with my ribs. It was painful and I had to strain to catch my breath. The next day because I was having a hard time breathing, I went to the hospital. They said my ribs were just bruised. We fished the rest of the tide and when the wind came up we headed back to the dock. Right now in 2011 with the striped bass contest still on, I would need a fish bigger than 47 pounds in order for me to even consider keeping it. Most all the fish we catch are released unless we are in the contest. So far this year I have an 81 pounder, 61 and a 47 pound striped bass. I won the "On the Water" contest last year and the title "Angler of the Year." I am thinking to fish Martha's Vineyard's contest next year to see what goes on there. I hear Yo-Yoing is a method of altering your bait and is banned at Martha's Vineyard. I am just learning about it; sounds interesting for non-tournament fishing.

A look back

I had a chance with a football scholarship to attend any major university in the country. I was an All-American high school football selection at linebacker, standing 6 foot 4 about 240 pounds but I went to the University of Rhode Island because I wanted to fish. Although opportunities to try out for the professional football teams were offered, I decided to go a different route. My brother went to Yale and played football and baseball and finally graduated as a 2nd lieutenant. He is a decorated veteran of the Gulf War and now an executive for the Nike Corporation. Both he and his wife are retired Marine officers. My cousin, Casey Pavano, a lawyer has also been a promoter of my endeavors and for our family's business.

I have owned several boats. When I was 12 years old my first one was made by Mr. Brockway from Lyme, Connecticut. I watched him build it in his yard. It was 17 feet long, all wood with a 5 hp Evinrude motor. I paid for it by trapping muskrats from the local river, about 600 of them during the season. I scanned and stretched out each one of them, placed them in a cooler and sold a whole batch to a local fur buyer. In those days because they were cleaned and stretched I got $12.50 each. This was payment for the boat.

A party and then the weigh in

By 10 PM the wind picked up and we were headed to the marina. At that time of the evening everything was shut down, there was no place to weigh my fish.so we went to Bills and had a party, maybe too much of a party. About 1 AM I went home with the fish. When I weighed it at home with my digital scale that goes to 120 pounds, it read 82 pounds. I put ·it on ice and waited for the morning. As I iced it down I noticed some monofilament dangling out of its mouth. It wasn't mine. The fish must have broken it off some time ago. This leader looked fairly new. I bet someone lost the record fish quite recently. Looking further into its mouth I noticed some rusty hooks. This cow had outwitted at least 2 or 3 anglers. Lucky she didn't do it to me. The fish was a 54 inches long and had a 35 inch girth. With its black stripes and multicolored glimmering scales, the fish looked absolutely beautiful in the twilight of that early evening. A magnificent fish.

Greg, this reminds me of a classical fishing story

The story of Moby Dick and Capt. Ahab (book by Herman Melville).

This world record bass meandered the coastal waters of the east coast for decades battling storms, foraging for food, and avoiding red tides, fatal commercial nets and 2 to 3 million striped bass anglers with fishing rods. Greg, like Moby Dick and Capt. Ahab chased the exclusive world record bass, month after month, week after week, night after night also for many, many years. Their ocean paths crossed on August 4, 2011 about 8 PM. This time no broken leader, no rusty hook, no frazzled fishing line, no wimpy rod, no fragile reel but a dedicated, passionate big bass angler whose meticulous preparation made this event almost predictable, just like the meeting of the whale Moby Dick and Capt. Ahab.

*The fish was out of the water from 8 PM to midnight that August 4. It was in the boat while everyone was taking pictures and I was in the tavern celebrating with my friends. I was uncertain my scale was correct therefore I called Jack at the weighing station to get there early, "I had something I wanted to show you." I told him it was a fish, a big fish, a gigantic fish. He believed me because over the seasons I have brought in quite a few 60 pound fish. His place was also a weighing station for the striped bass fishing contest. That morning I slept through 8 AM although Jack arrived at 6 AM at his place. In the meantime a lot of people were at the weighing station awaiting my arrival and this fish. The word that this could be a new world record striped bass spread like wildfire. Here I arrived hung over, couldn't breathe and my ribs ached. Jack had his scale already when I arrived. It was a digital scale quite similar to mine. There were a whole lot of people most of whom I didn't know. The scale **read 81.88 pounds**. Jack turned around and went inside to the telephone. I didn't know at that time who he had called. Jack came back while the people were still taking pictures of the fish. He took the fish off the scale and made a thorough inspection, like he always does. In the meantime I waited by the truck because I didn't feel well. He came back out and announced "everything looked good," nothing was wrong. I told him to hold the fish while I went to the hospital, my ribs felt like they were broken and I was about to get sick. I changed my mind and took the fish back to the truck and then Rick, a fishing buddy of mine, called and said he wanted to see this monster fish. He asked me to stop by so he could see it. The fish was in the cooler as I pulled into his place. It's right down the street from the marina. As I entered his house his phone rang. It was Jack. He said, "Don't go anywhere, get the fish back here. Newsmen, magazine reps and radio men are coming to see the fish, NBC, CBS." I said "I don't care I'm too tired, I've got to get some sleep." Rex said, "Don't go, I won't let you go, this is a big thing, you have to hang around." At this time I really didn't care it was just another big fish and I was tired, I was hurting and I couldn't care. Looking back I know I wasn't thinking clearly hence I took the easy way out. One a magazine writer from "On the Water" arrived at Jack's place looking for the fish. I went back with the fish and had a photo session and gave them a short story about the catch. Everyone admired the bass.*

With all the excitement and accolades I just wanted to let them know

I am probably one of the better striped bass fishermen. That's what is important to me not the money, gifts and stories. I don't care about anything else but I have been blessed with a certain mystic aurora as I leave the docks each night. Friends and strangers greet me in various ways. It's part of having the world record striped bass. That's okay I appreciate their gestures. I salute them back.

Maybe someday I'll write a book about everything.

IGFA -international Game and Fish Association- and past record holder

Although the IGFA contacted me by phone I never saw anyone. Jack, owner of the weighing station, must have handled this. They wanted 50 feet of my line with pictures of the rod, reel plus the leader and hook. I must have talked to the IGFA about 10 to 20 times concerning my fish. They would say I need this, I need that and then call back tomorrow and say I want this and I want that. The weighing scale had to be recertified in Hartford Connecticut by the agents of the IGFA. My scale was accurate to 100 pounds.

AI McReynolds, the previous record holder, called to congratulate me. We talked about baseball, football and everything including a little bit about what to do and not to do with the media. He should know if you read his story. AI McReynolds' son dropped by not too long ago and we had a good conversation about his dad, who is now retired and lives in Naples, Florida. We exchanged photos and had a good time. AI had given his son an autographed copy of him with his world record striped bass. I cherish this photo as much as my big bass. The story of my fish was highlighted in a news report on Good Morning America.

"On the Water" magazine wanted to take the fish but I refused to give it to them. I have a good relationship with the magazine and got this bold request resolved. It really wasn't a problem, I just wasn't going to give them the fish. The marine biologist at the

University of Rhode Island had the fish and they wanted to study it. I will do what I can to help study the life cycles of these fish.

Each time I motor out of the marina I'm followed by a group of my fellow fishermen in their own boats. Some wave at me, some hi-fi me and all follow me; it's the price of catching the world record striped bass. That's what the IGFA certificate says. It's right next to my fish, both hanging on the wall in my home.

I have room for another one, but a little bigger.

PS: Greg's big bass as you may have guessed by now, wasn't luck. Preparation was the key to his success. A few years ago Greg tested a new fishing lure he invented. With an

acoustic microphone lowered it near the bottom of his fishing area, he recorded the sounds of one of the striped bass favorite foods; lobster. The sounds were in the 47 to 67 dB range. With time and effort he developed a sinker that when in motion vibrated and produced sound between 47 to 67 dbs. Sound travels very well under water as you and the US Navy knows and so do the bass. This "lobster like" 'vibration produced the sound that drew the bass to the eel about 36 inches from the sinker. If you read that Greg caught another monster bass with an eel, the acoustic sinker is the other part of the bait. He called the sinker "Rattlesinker".

Greg says bass are near-sighted at night and the lobster feed at that time. He fishes 40 minutes around slack time where the current is no more than Y2 knot. The lazy bass will look for easy, slow moving prey. The lobster fits that menu but the eel will also do. There are four slack times per 24 hours.

His acoustic (no batteries) sinkers can be found on his Web site: www.worldrecordstripercompany. Prices, video, contact information are available at the Web site. There is a patent on this product.

CHAPTER 8

SUNSET-SUNRISE

Finally TC and I started to do some surf fishing. Next morning we started out bait fishing for it gave us time to talk over what has happened in the last 48 hours. We didn't give a hoot if we caught anything. Never checked the bait for 4 hours. Left the rods in the sand while we went to lunch. We were still enchanted about Kate, her early life, with her mom Katie, school, adventures in L.A. How the outcome would have been different if he had known earlier. Life paths are not always straight.

I stayed for the rest of my vacation with TC. We visited his "hot-spot", caught enough bass to earn my badge as an experienced surf jockey. We visited again the old tackle shops that TC knew in the area, the radio station and newspaper. Surf fishing was great. We got wet, salty, sunburn and sore shoulders when we switched to throwing tins and plugs. We fished days and into the night. I felt like a kid again anticipating the next great adventure in the surf. TC kept up with me but we were both glad our fishing success came to an end. I was looking forward to see my wife and renew our life. TC will begin a new life path with Kate and his grandkids. We both had a great vacation. What more can you ask from a surf fishing vacation. Sun, sea and being part of a new found love. Sounds like a striped bass romance with all the necessary ingredients.

Striped Bass World Record Stories

Gregg Myerson striped bass worldwide all tackle record story is contained in this book. I have other striped bass records stories in other books I have written. There were some stories that could not be obtained since the anglers have passed on or cannot be found or their story is not for publication.

When G. Myerson caught his 81.88 pound striped bass several stories of 70+ pound bass were directed to the trash bin. These wonderful stories lost their importance for the moment. They may arise sometime in the future but not now. Why should we care about them? The fact that such rare events have occurred in our sport, we should all relish the accomplishment of the fisherman or woman. Something that should be shared not retired. Records show that few big bass survived to such an old age. The odds one could be caught is enormous. The odds that one angler would be at the right place, the right time and with the right equipment is beyond comprehension. Just ask the angler if he expected such luck? Many fishermen spend a life time seeking such a fish.

Contained in the next pages are the stories of past record striped bass that were or are still records acknowledged by the IGFA. The older the story the more accomplished was the angler by landing the fish. Comparing the equipment of 50 years ago consisting of bamboo rods, linen and silk line, reels developed by watchmakers to today's carbon fiber rods, braided line and precision reels, it's a wonder big bass were ever landed. May you be blessed with such luck!

These stories may have appeared in other books in part or whole.

Robert a Rochetta

Striped bass 76 pounds} Montauk Point,
New York, July 17, 1981

IGFA World Line Class Record: 50 pounds -line class record

Since I was a young boy, I have been in love with Long Island waterways. They have played an important part in my life. While fishing with my father, we used to stalk many species of fish that swam in the unusual contours of the North Shore. Learning and growing by his side, I hoped to someday be the fisherman he was. The years passed and I lost my dad. Now I would be fishing alone but I remembered all that he taught me. As I got older, I also fished harder and more often leaving no stone unturned. I read every fishing article I could get my hands on. There was a yearning in me to be fishing constantly. It became a passion.

There came a time when all my efforts were directed to seek the most elusive of all fish, the striped bass. Little did I realize the time and toll it would take to master the catching up; Old Linesilders. It was no longer the school fish that interested me but the legendary cows swam so exclusively along with the Island.

In the early 1970s, I bought a 4 wheel drive vehicle. Now with mobility I could venture further along the beaches in search of those big bass. Cruising the island's shores, I met some of the finest fishermen I have ever known. Collecting and practicing each technique they taught me, I began to perfect their methods and develop my own. My surf casting days had produced some fish into the 30 pound range, yet l was still not satisfied. Watching the birds working beyond the reach of my casts, I realized the need to extend my efforts from the beach to a territory beyond the breakers.

At that unable to afford any sleek fishing boat, I settled for a homemade wooden boat. This cost me more in time and money to put it together. The whole was soon replaced by a used fiberglass one. It was with this boat"," The Rainbow11 that my fishing goals were finally fulfilled. I caught many big stripers on her including several over 50 pounds.

My primary fishing grounds were from Plum Gut and Orient Point along the chain of islands to Fishers Island. In 1977 I headed south to Montauk Point to investigate reports of big bass. With my fishing buddy, Bill Peggy Collins, we confirmed those reports and saw the potential for large and more varied catches. Montauk became my home port.

It was while fishing off Montauk, in an area called Great Eastern, I was blessed with the ultimate catch I often dreamed but never really expected it. On July 17, 1981shortly after the partial eclipse of a full, moon, I landed the largest bass I ever saw. It was preceded by a frustrating evening of inactivity. Tired and bored my 13 year old companion, Eddie Turner, fell asleep in my boat. My fishing partner, John Alberda, in his fishing boat, was fishing nearby. We would take turns looking for bass at different depths on our instruments but to no avail. Finally the word of encouragement came. "Hey, Bob got one in the boat John caught the first fish of the night. It was now well into the outgoing tide and I was hoping John's catch would signal the start of "the bite". I waited for my eel to give me the hell tail sign that the fish were starting to feed. It was the radio that again told me of more fish. John had another. He spotted more on his recorder and told me to get over there. I left my unproductive spot and motored over towards John where I started my first drift. Viewing the bottom through my line recorder, I also saw a fish. I was the hunter stalking his quarry. As we drifted together, my frustrations was mounting. In the moonlight the bent arc of John's rod told me his next catch was in progress.

I question John on what was his technique and he told me to relax and use the same old technique— two turns off the bottom and then bow to the fish. Bowing to the fish meant hold your rod high over the horizon and as you feel the hit, lower your tip. Free the spool gently until you feel the line taut, then strike the fish. Several other regulars showed up to join in this drift. Within moments I could hear the whip of all the rods setting up. Then I heard the familiar grunts as they suck home their gaff and lifted a larger bass into their boats.

As I made my next drift, I noticed on my recorder a large mark slightly off the bottom and at the top of a There was no doubt, a larger bass was feeding. Two drifts later she was still there. It was now my turn. I felt the eel give the signal as it tried to flee from the feeding bass. Finally I got the hit. Bowing to the fish, I readied myself to set the hook. The line started to peel off my Ambassador real smoothly and steadily. I locked the spool. I could feel the line becoming taut. Pointing the rod straight at the fish, I was prepared to set the hook. As the line started peeling with more speed than I expected, it burned my thumb. I then struck the fish. Unable to keep enough pressure on the spool, it backlashed. Upset that things were not happening as usual, I attempted to untangle the mess. I could not accept the fact that I might lose my first fish of the night. As she pulled each loop in the snarl grew tighter. I knew that shortly it will end in a sudden snap at the knot. Slack out, loops drawn tightly, my arms and rod went straight out into the water. My knees were tucked under gunwales as I stretch my body out and over rail. I knew it was a large fish because of the tremendous pull it exhibited.

Out of fear of losing the fish, I knew I had to do something. One hand on the rod butt, one hand clinching the line so the mono would no longer pull at the back lash and knot, I lifted the rod with all my might. As the rod tip dove down, it became a tug of war. Finally raising the tip high enough to clear the rail, I backed up pulling the line in as far as I could. I worked the rod back over my head and then lowered the tip and reel in as fast as I could. As the fish tugged and pulled me back to the rail, I tightened it down on the drag and this got me a few more turns on the reel. I repeated this technique knowing I had but a few feet to give the fish because of the knot. The bass made another run. I gained more line and my confidence gradually returned. My feeling of comfort did not last for long as the fish ran out all the line l had retrieved. The tightness of the drag seemed to have vanished. I was again down to the knot. My worry returned.

I wanted this fish. She was big. I could feel her weight as she displayed all the characteristics of a record fish. I again returned to my first technique. Lift high the rod, moved backwards and reel like hell as I moved forward.

Now I chanced ripping the hook from her mouth, rather than getting to that knot one more time. It was an instant replay.

My rod tip was limber and this was the first fish on this new rod. The rod was balanced and it absorbed the pounding and pulling of her fight. Contrary to most large fish, they usually run twice but this one was now going for her third run. I estimated this was at least a 50 pound fish. I thought to myself it must be fouled hook? If so, how much more of this fight could go on before something else would go wrong and I would lose her. Would the hook finally pull out? Would the line break?

Once again regaining line, I could feel her slow up as I worked her towards the boat. This was the longest fight I ever had with a bass and for the first time she broke the surface. I could see her 30 feet from the boat. He fin cut like a knife through a watermelon as her silver blue body glistened in the moonlight. Her pull was not as strong and my drag was holding as I reeled in. Then a slap of her tail and again she dove almost to the bottom. I did not believe her power and determination. She leveled out, I hoped that she would soon be mine. Shortly after this l saw her again, this time by the side of the boat. She was a belly up and fatigued after the 15 minute battle. The fish appeared almost helpless as it floated in the water next to the boat. Alerted by all the commotion young Eddie stood there waiting for directions. I shouted, "Eddie, give me the gaff." I told him, "It was a big one." I positioned the rod against the rail, grabbed the leader, and then struck home with the gaff. As I lifted the heavy fish, the handle of gaff broke. I fell back into the boat, as the fish slipped back into the water. I was prepared to go swimming to recover this fish. As she sank below the surface only a few feet away, I was able to grab what was left of the gaff. I pulled the fish back to the boat, put one hand under the gills and kept one hand on the gaff. I lifted the fish with every ounce of my strength over the real and into the boat. Eddie and I gazed at her in amazement. "What is it", Eddie asked? I told him it was the biggest cow bass I had ever seen.

In total excitement and like a rookie at catching his one big bass, I responded to the radio to tell my friend, John. Calmly he said, "Good now get back up here and catch some more." I returned to young Eddie and said, "Now it's your turn." Shortly afterwards Eddie boated a 35 pounder.

After daybreak the fishing done for the night, it was back to the dock for breakfast and weigh the fish. Unable to remove her from the boat by hand, we needed to use a pulley to lift her up to the dock. John seeing the fish for the first time gave me a nod of confidence and said, "I will weigh her for you over there." Surrounded by several of the local fishermen, some of the best bass fisherman on long Island, John announced, "Seventy five pounds, the world record." The commotion began. With the help of Capt.

Frank Brad Locke of the boat "Hurry Up", Capt. Jack Passie of "Windy" and Carl Dannenberg of the Montauk Marine basin, the paperwork for the IGFA was completed. The official weight was not 75 but 76 pounds.

The next few hours were filled with excitement, reporters, photographs and well- wishers. The fish was taken to Eastern Taxidermy in Farmingville for mounting. The excitement continued into the next week and congratulations came from across the country.

Several days later, after the taxidermist work was completed, I could not see discarding this special fish as garbage. Accompanied by young Eddie, I packed the now distorted corpus of the fish into my boat and returned her to the waters off Montauk where she had passed for the last 25 years. As she disappeared below the surface, young Eddie asked, "Do you think I will ever catch one that big?" I answered, "Eddie, it could have been anyone of the fishermen there that night that could have caught her. We all paid our dues. I was the lucky one this time. Work hard and learn as much as you can. Put in your time and one day I'm sure the fish you catch will be bigger than mine."

After almost 25 years, I still thank God for having giving me this fish. I am getting older and it is harder for me to endure the sacred moments of night fishing. I have been successful with catching fish during the day and evenings, with an assortment of fishing methods. The mystique and beauty that often comes on at those late night tides will always be part of my life and memories. The striped bass is a magnificent creature, it has altered many people's lives. It has become more than a fish to me, kind of a sacred beast that I respect and honor. Someday when my ashes leave on the outgoing tide during a full moon, I hope a school of stripers will escort them out to sea.

Rosa A Webb

Striped Bass 64.5 pounds, August 14,
1960, Truro, Massachusetts

IGFA Woman's World Record- all classes

On August 14, 1960 I caught the 64 ½ pound striped bass off North Truro, Massachusetts.

My husband and I motored out about ½ mile from the beach, in order to catch some live mackerel. Likewise, our dose friends Jack and Kay Townsend did the same. little did we know what would unfold memorable day?

We knew the bass were either hiding at the edge of the sandbars or just below the patches of floating seaweed. This brown seaweed like vegetation is present throughout the Cape during the summer but recedes during the fall. Some would call it snot grass. It was hard to realize that in those days you could catch forty- 40 pound bass on the same day and on the same beach {1961). As the seasons progressed they also started to catch 50 pound bass. David caught several them in 1958. They used surf plugs like the Reverse Atoms and other similar plugs. Saltwater artificials were limited. Sometimes when the spearing were running they would net a bunch of them, string them up on an 8/0 O/Shaughnessy hook and catch these lunkers. Jack and Kay's two sons also landed some of these large bass using a string of spearing.

It was Sunday morning, very little wind and a nice warm day for mid- August. There were a few boaters motoring the sandbars from Race Point south. David and I, placed ourselves just behind the breakers that were about 50 yards from the shore. With my Harneli fiberglass rod and Penn 140 reel (full of 45 pound test braided line), little did I know that this line rating was way off.

After submitting the terminal tackle to the IGFA, they tested the line and said the line was not rated at 45 pound test but in the low 30 pound range. This permitted me to break the previous woman's record for theW 15 KG line class (33 pounds), which I still hold today, 46 years later.

The mackerel was hooked in the back of the rear dorsal fin and sent on its way. With the surf rod and reel in hand, "Whack" the mackerel was airborne. In a few seconds the mono line just screamed off the real. Fifty three pounds later David helped me get this bass into the boat. Not bad for a start.

Another 2 pound mackerel with an 8/0 hook was sent off. The tide moved us closer to the beach and David decided for safety to anchor the boat. Over went the little anchor and it held while calmness settled over the both of us. Not for long. "Whack", the mackerel was airborne. Again in a few seconds, which seemed like a few minutes, the mono line peeled off the reel at a rapid rate. I hauled back at Dave's command and off we went, the boat, the anchor and us. Yes, the anchor to.

It was about 25-30 minutes of give and take. David using the oars tried to keep the boat's motor from fraying the line. The bass swam right, then left, then in and out. One thing about striped bass, you never quite know what they will do. The fish felt like a good one, yet looking back, I think a 40 pounder probably would out fight and outlast most 60 pounders. They are all lean and young: just like a 40-year old man who will outlast, a 60-year-old man.

I finally got the bass close to the boat. Years of experience cautioned me not to be so fast with this "endgame." My husband would rather get it over with quickly. His technique is to hook on, haul in and board now. Being a woman I have a more delicate touch. We finally boarded the bass without much trouble.

Kay Townsend, my best friend, had just caught a 63 ½ pound

bass about 2 hours before me. Same technique, boat, rod, reef and mackerel. She left for the weighing station while we were fishing. We were pretty sure her catch would be a world-class line record for a woman. It was and the proper IGFA documents were completed. Upon her return with her good news, I presented her with my catch, just 1 pound more than hers. My bass also won the Worcester Striper Derby prize in 1960. Kay's record bass lasted for only 2 hours but we are still friends. David also caught a 64 ½ pound bass that season. There were many big bass caught that fabulous year.

About 3 years earlier, Kay had a similar experience. She had the world record class for striped bass one day and another woman broke it the next day. Two for two. I told my best friend I hated to be the two. She forgave the fish first and then me. My record bass does not exist, since we sold it like all the other bass. I have plenty of pictures but no fish. If I knew my record would have lasted so long, I would have had it mounted.

In those great "big bass" days (40/50 pounders) of the late 50s and 60s, we caught so many big bass that we felt any day someone else would break my record fish. Time went on and either the big bass population declined or woman fishing for them declined. Maybe both happened.

As of 2007 Rosa Webb still holds the woman's 30 pound line class record for striped bass per the IGFA.

Steven R. Thomas

Striped Bass, 66.75 pounds, Bradley Beach, N.J. Nov., 1979

IGFA World Record-12 Pound Class

Interview with Steve Thomas on May 30, 2006 at a coffee shop in Plymouth Meeting, Pennsylvania.

Usually my family and I would go where we could do some fishing every holiday. This was how I received my angling education while fishing the Delaware River.

I got married after college and my first job required that I move out of the Philadelphia area to Bradley Beach, New Jersey. My apartment was less than one block from the beach. Saltwater fishing was a different experience for me at this time because all my past fishing was done in freshwater. I got the bug and I loved it. I worked for a chemical specialty company some miles away and I did not know the area but the beach was out my front door.

As saltwater fishing was rather new to me, I try to learn from other men fishing off the jetties of Bradley Beach. My wife and I would spend some time on the beach and I would spend a bit of time fishing when the beach area was free of bathers. I would try the inlets as well as the jetties. Fishing after dinner was a habit of mine especially in 1979 when I caught the big fish. Sometimes I would get up at 4:30 in the morning in order to get on the jetty prior to sunrise and then back to apartment to get ready for work. I loved it, of course. I had prepared all my gear night before.

When I left the apartment I had my gear on; waders, jetty spikes, gaff, miners light and my fishing pouch. It was about two years' worth of fishing experience on beach and jetty before I caught big one. In 1979 I committed myself to fish as often as I could. i would fish early morning and late evening.

117

My experience taught me with striped bass you have a much chance of success by fishing in the evening tide than daylight.

Most of the time I would fish the Brindley Avenue jetty because I knew it well and it was right out my front door. On weekends during the daytime I might try other jetties and nearby inlets and even try flounder fishing at Shark River Inlet. There was a group of Pennsylvania fishermen who came down on weekends and I got to know them well. They were about my age and I looked up to them because they were dedicated anglers. They would fish all night. There van was properly equipped with rod holders, extra fishing rod/reels as well as places to sleep. I was a little jealous of their equipment and they were a little jealous of my opportunity to fish every day. Although my jetty bag was mostly filled with Red Fins, the big fish was court on a rigged eels, the first eel I ever tried. It was a dead rigged eel that a tackle shop in Long Branch, New Jersey made. I went back to him after I caught the big fish to tell him of my success. There was about a half inch of lead located towards the head of the eel. This added weight gave me the ability to make a decent cast. The eel was about 18 inches long, had a hook in its head and another about way down the body.

I use a lot of excuses with my wife in order to participate in my fishing passion. We did not have any children at this time so this allowed me to do quite a bit of fishing. My wife worked as a waitress in the evening's hence this gave me lots of time to fish; sometimes half an hour stretched into a few hours. During the summer we spent more time together on the beach.

Our first move was to Red Bank, New Jersey for about one year and then to Bradley Beach, New Jersey for 4 years but I did not start jetty fishing until our move to Bradley Beach.

I really love this kind fishing. Being close to the ocean gave me an opportunity to be there when fish arrived. I saw several fishermen catch goods size bass and it encouraged me to do the same. I learned as much as I could watching them and then use their same tactics. I would watch the fishermen they anticipate where the school of baitfish would be and then get into position before the bass arrived. That early success courage me to do the same. I learned what equipment they used; rod, reel, line, lure techniques used to catch big bass.

Author: "Steve, what do you remember about the big day you caught that big fish?"

It was the day after Halloween; I believe it was Thursday, midweek. I didn't have a chance to fish on Halloween day so I felt that I need to get on the jetty night. When I came home from work my wife said "We're going out to dinner tonight with friends." I did not know we had an appointment. I hummed and a hawed about not wanting to go. She relented so I hiked to the beach while my wife went to our dinner appointment by herself. Good wife.

I had worked the whole day, had a quick dinner and it was just past 7 o'clock before I went to the jetty. By late October it was already dark but the air temperature was quite warm, probably over 60°.

In the moonlight I saw kids playing on the beach and it reminded me how nice the evening was for this time of year. The bright moon was partially full and the quite surf shimmered in the moonlight as the gentle waves lapped against the rocks. I had my light and the wooden gaff handily hung from my chest waders. I had made the gaff out of one end of a flounder net so I had both net and gaff on one stick. The whole contraption was about 5 feet long. Slowly I made my way out on the jetty and noticed one fisherman already there.

I think the other fisherman was casting a plug. My rod and reel was not expensive, something you could buy at most any sports store. After my big fish they teased me about the simple rod and reel I use to catch this record fish. It goes to show you luck plays a big part in this game. Later the IGFA required a picture of the rod, reel, line and me together with the fish.

The fellow in front of me was on the south side of the jetty and an order not to interfere with him, I moved to the north side. I said hello to him and he in return said hello to me. I said "I'm Steven" and he replied, "I'm Bob." We were courteous to each other since we were fishing on the same jetty and in close proximity to each other. I was using a rigged eel as described before and I was retrieving as slowly as possible, as instructed. The eel spent most of its time on the bottom of the sand. As it approached the jetty, I would instinctively raise it rapidly in order to avoid the rocks. Moonlight helped me when to make the decision. I had previously positioned myself so there was a slight void between rocks where I could maneuver the eel and lift it clear. It was simply common sense. I think it was pretty dose to high tide. This big fish must have been 2 or 3 feet out from the rocks when I started my quick retrieve to avoid hanging the in the rocks. 'Whack,' it startled me. The rod was instantly jerked 45° towards the splash of the bass was right in front of me. The bass took off and sped towards the other jetty northme. In New Jersey jetties can be hundreds of yards apart.

Going, going and going. I left the drag alone because I needed time to think what to do as she kept taking out line. This gave me some time to worry about what was going on. If this fish keeps going, am I going to run out of line or wind up near some rocks and have the line cut? A quickly looked at the reel in the moonlight showed me half my line was already gone and she was still going strong just as fast as she started. I was in trouble and worried about how much line I had left and what other options I had. I thought about increasing the drag. I think she must have run to the next to jetty. I had just put on 300 yards of 10 pound test line on the reel. I think she must have taken at least two thirds of it before she stopped. I left the drag alone.

After the first big run I was gaining more line than losing. The several shorter runs indicated there was not much fight left in this fish. I wanted to ensure that she was entirely spent by the time she got to my jetty with its surrounding rocks. I estimate the total time about 30 minutes because of her long run and my desire to play it to total exhaustion.

I yelled to Bob, the other fisherman, to put his light on so we could spot the fish. As the fish came dose to the jetty, I could see it was pretty well spent. It was a beautiful looking fish, pure white body, lots of blue green colors shining in the moonlight. Other stripers I've caught did not look nearly as beautiful as this one. Bob pointed his light as 1 maneuvered the fish towards the void in the rocks. We were about 5 to 10 feet above the water and the fish was floating down below us. Bob went down into the rocks with my handmade I didn't want to bring the fish too dose to the rocks before Bob was set with the gaff. Bob got the gaff into the fish but as soon as he pulled on it, the long wooden handle broke. Right then I started to go down into the rocks after this fish. Holding my rod in one hand, I maneuvered myself into the rocks at the same time trying to keep fish in front of me. I got my hand under the gills. This was the great moment. This was a fantastic moment. If it goes swimming again, I am going with it. Let's go, I am ready but this fish was spent.

With fish in one hand and rod in the other, I started to make my way up the rocks. After a few steps i threw my rod to Bob, now high on the jetty rocks. The front hook of the eel had hooked the fish. I unhooked the eel and hauled the fish to the next rock above me with my hands still in its gills. The fish was heavy and 1 did this several times before I got to the top of the jetty. It was a long, long walk down the jetty back to the shoreline. I was physically and emotionally exhausted as well as the fish. I kept asking myself how much did this fish weigh? I guessed about 70 pounds. It was after 9 PM by now and there wasn't any place to it weigh it. We tossed the fish into Bob's car and tried to find a tackle shop that was open. It is not a popular time for tackle shops to be open in late October. So I went to a store and bought some bags of ice and put the fish into the bathtub at home with the ice.

No water with the ice, only the fish and ice.

My wife came home and I didn't say anything. I let her go to the bathroom and she almost fainted. The fish filled the entire bathtub.

I had a tough time sleeping that night. The adrenaline kept me up thinking about this memorable experience. At that time the world record was about 72 pounds and I thought this fish was dose to that weight. I could hardly sleep a wink.

I woke up early the next day and found a shop that had a certified scale so I could officially record the fish. I called ahead and told them I caught a big bass last night and needed to have it weighed. The shop was in the harbor in Belmar where the commercial boats dock. I brought the fish down and I was surprised to find out the word got around and there was a big crowd around the tackle shop. Their owner of the shop thought this might be a record fish and he called the local newspapers. The newspaper also sent a photographer to take pictures of the fish. I often wondered if the fish lost a few pounds while sitting in the bathtub and could have dried out before the weigh in. I used 10 pound test line because I liked the way it cast. I think my fish still holds the 12 pound line class striped bass record.

The Asbury Park Press newspaper took pictures and I spoke to a news man on the telephone but not in person. He wrote a nice article and also mentioned it in the weekly edition. It also made the Outdoor Life Magazine because they were looking for a fish for their "Big Fish Records" edition. There weren't any television broadcast about this fish.

When I tell people about the catch, many are surprised that it was caught so close to the jetty. I've caught several fish dose to the jetty rocks and have found a lot of them had small crabs in their stomachs hence the reason they probably came to the rocks.

In certain ways this fish has changed my life. I have become the local expert for striped bass fishing amongst my family and friends. They usually set high hopes for success whenever I join them. It's sometimes difficult to meet their expectations but that's okay. I continued to fish the Brindley Street jetty for two more years before I changed jobs and moved back to the Philadelphia area in 1981.

Probably this big fish helped me in my job interviews because they assumed that I did something very well even though it had nothing to do with chemistry. It may have influenced them because I did get the position. This fish put me in the world class record book and it is still there. Some of my fishing friends became jealous because of my catch but that's life.

The IGFA sent me a certificate saying that it was the biggest striped bass caught that year.

A lot of my fishing friends old and new thought I was too young to catch such a big fish. I had not put in sufficient time to be rewarded with such a catch. Looking back into the past, I did put in a lot of times during those years; I got up at 4:30AM, back to fishing after dinner, late in the evening, etc.

I did it in only a couple of years and that proves that you don't have to have 50 years of fishing the jetties to get lucky, you just have to be lucky.

Wilfred Fontaine

Striped bass 68 pounds, Charlestown,
Rhode Island, October 3, 1965

IGFA World Record - 20 pound line class

It was October 3, 1965 and Wilfred Fontaine was competing in the R. J. Schaefer Saltwater Fishing contest. He decided to try his luck at one of his favorite spots in Green Hili, Rhode Island by casting out to a small sandbar where bass like to hide. The weather was terrible. The wind was up. The surf was up. From time to time the fast moving clouds outlining the angry surf. The following is from his daughter's scrapbook and her memories of her father.

Joe Pimentle was with him but was fishing in a different area. He was battling the weather just as Wilfred was. They started fishing about 5 PM and about 10 PM had spent 5 hours without a strike. He was about to call it a night and go find Joe but on his next cast all of the sudden the bass grabbed the eel. Though years of experience as a member of the Scituate Saltwater Anglers "Sixty Pound Club" and the "Nifty 50 Club" told him this was a pretty good fish, maybe another 50 pound.

For 25 minutes he struggled fighting this fish. It was give and take with the big bass doing most of the taking. Pump and pull, then pull and pump. Wilfred tried to anticipate its every move in order to stay in front of it. The moon had slipped away by now and it was only the taut of the line against a rod that led him move to the fish. The bass ran straight out with its first run and he was concerned if it would stop. The line was on a Pen 700 spinning reel attach to a Lamiglas surf rod with 20 pound Ashway Magic Mono line. The line was running out too fast. It finally turned and swam with the current and he ran with it. Thank god it slowed down giving Wilfred a chance to guide the fish to the surf line. The waves were increasing in height and the wind was starting to blow even harder. Finally after about 20 minutes battling the fish, it was close enough to attempt to gaff it, but the fish still had plenty of fight left. Every time the fish was brought in close, it would sense the surf, turn and head back out into the white water.

It had been a long day of fishing and Wilfred was getting tired but this bass kept up the fight.

Five times he carefully nursed the bass close to the surf line. Each time it sense the breakers and took off again. What a great fish! Who was going to tire out first, she or Wilfred? How many chances will he get to land this fish? The line could break at any moment. The bass could spit out the eel as she twisted and turned in the surf. Wilfred needed help. Just then, as these thoughts were racing through his mind, his fishing buddy Joe came over to see if he had any luck. He asked, "Will do you need any help?" He was on time. Finally on the sixth attempt Joe was able to successfully gaff the lunker in between waves. With no idea the fish was a record and even though it was exhausting, Joe and Wilfred decided to continue fishing. The fish was placed on the sand and Wilfred went on to catch a 50 pound bass that night.

The next morning they finally decided that it was time to go to the weighing station. When the fish was weighed, they were stunned to hear the officials say it was 68 pounds. It had tied a world record. Even though Wilfred was advised that if he had brought the fish to be weighed immediately, it would have record. Wilfred was still ecstatic about his trophy catch. The bass was a 53 1/2 inches long and had a girth of 32 1/2 inches. He caught another 60 lbs. 9 oz. bass later on in October, near Narragansett, Rhode Island. Don't ask exactly where. It was a good year for 60 pounders.

He was so proud of the fish as well as exhausted that he even

125

took the next day off. Wilfred met with Evening Journal staff photographer S. Carroll and had a photo taken that was published around the country. Carroll was so thrilled to see the big fish that he begged to have his photo taken with it. No problem, it was the biggest bass caught that year. Everybody had a chance to be photographed with it.

There are conflicting reports about where the fish was actually caught. Many of the printed articles that were published immediately after the fish was caught, stated that it was caught at Green Hilt, Rhode Island while others including the plaque on the amount of fish, stated that it was caught at Charlestown, Rhode Island. This was because, being the competitive fisherman, he didn't want others to learn where he had really caught the fish. He did it wanted to share one of his best spots hence he purposefully changed the location to Charlestown to mislead others. That's fair in love, war and fishing, especially fishing.

Wilfred had the fish professionally mounted by Jeanne Martel of South Attleboro, Massachusetts. She did a fantastic job with the display. The fish was even displayed at the Springfield Fair, Springfield, Massachusetts in the sporting booth operated by F and M Schaefer Brewing Company. In a letter from F and M Schaefer Brewing Company, the public relations director, advised us that Jack Woolner took movies of the mounted fish displayed at the fairs booth and used the footage on the TV show, "Dateline Boston" on February 1, 1966.

"Field and Stream Magazine" in March 1966 awarded him a certificate and pin for this accomplishment. Penn Reels awarded him a new reef as well as a congratulatory letter. F and M Schaffer Brewing Company awarded him an honorary certificate for his caches in 1962 and 1966 as part of their Salt Water Fishing Contest. Likewise Ashway Line and Twine Manufacturing Company and Lamiglas Rods did the same.

The mounted trophy was proudly displayed on the Fontaine's the living room wall until they moved into a retirement center. The fish was donated to the Snug Harbor Marina where his fishing buddies hung out. To this day the striper is still on display at the Marina.

Wilfred lost his battle with cancer at age 75 in 1994. He continued to fish almost to the end. His wife Rita fondly recalled her life has a "fishermen's widow" and how she would watch Wilfred and his buddies take off for a day of fishing. They would be gone all day and often all night and she never knew the time they would return. She even admits that he did a little fishing on the morning of their wedding day. Just a little. She was still supportive of his hobby and proud when he brought home the big ones as well as the smaller ones but especially when he brought back himself.

Authors note: Prior to July 1, 1970, the IGFA asked for part of the line that had been used to catch fish. The specifications as to its line strength were assumed as the listed in the manufacturer's catalog. After this date, all lines were tested as submitted with the application for a record and even past lines were tested to their strength and adjustments made to the records, if necessary.

Anton Stezko,
World Record Striped Bass

73.0 pounds, Nov 2,1981

I met Anton (Tony) Stezko back in 2006 in Orleans Massachusetts. I heard about a world record striped bass he caught and I was interested in his story. Recently a friend of mine told me Tony had died. I never got his complete story about this big bass but I am going to try to remember what he told me about the event that night.

It was about noon June 13, 2006 when I walked into the print shop in Orleans, Cape Cod. This tall lanky, chiseled faced man was rushing back and forth trying to finish a print job that was due at 4 PM. It was for a long time customer and Tony didn't want him to try some of the new competitors that had recently arrived. They must have heard of his good work because they located not very far away from his shop. Tony had been there for over 20 years printing all the needs for the growing industries in this area. Having to share some of the increasing work, gave him time to develop a new career; that of a saltwater fishing guide. Early evenings to near midnight it was time to lay the copy down and teach him some novice striped bass anglers the techniques of striped bass fishing.

Even with all his work demanding his attention he was kind enough to show me his trophy bass as they hung along the wall. Three {3} monsters including his 73 pounds plus two (2) others nearly the same size were hung from the rafters as well as 100 plugs all carved by him. All sizes and all colors. I felt rushed chatting with him but I understood his need to "get the presses rolling." 11 Drop back tomorrow and let's continue our conversation," he said. I did and listen to hisstory and learned "if only I could have seen the future in 1982." Reflecting back I presume Tony had miss the opportunity to get in the plug manufacturing business especially making saltwater plugs.

He said, "I started fishing when I was a little kid with my dad along the New Jersey coast. I was about 4 or 5 years old when we went to Sandy Hook and he would hook the bait firmly because I could not cast very well at that age and he would also help me reel in the fish. This was surf fishing at Sandy Hook and I was hooked. I loved it. We fished from Sandy Hook to Long Branch to Asbury Park to Barnegat light in those years. There are many jetties along the coastline in this area of New Jersey and we climbed on lots of them.

Looking back at Fort Hancock military reminded me of Cape Cod. It is a beautiful place to fish from the sand. You want to go as far as you can to the rip located at the point of Sandy Hook. We used a beach buggy in those days to drive to the rip as well as Offices Beach. My sister also like to fish and was quite good at catching all kinds of species. When I moved to the Cape she came to the Cape and for many years fished with me.

My dad made his own fishing plugs. He was always making different models and taught me how to do the same. That is why today I probably have hundreds of wooden plugs as well as various eel lures. My father was a machinist and he always made his own fishing plugs because the machinery was at his disposal. Being a dedicated surf fisherman he was interested in finding new and better lures to catch fish. Back in those days, salt water plugs were a rarity. What few were around were fresh water clones.

We never caught any big fish at Sandy Hook but lots of medium size bass pounds, 20, 25, 30 pounds but I recall a friend of my dad caught a 60 pound bass in this same area. There were plenty of bluefish, weak fish as well as king fish, if the bass action slowed down.

When I was 16 we would drive to Rhode Island as well as Cape Cod to have some new fishing experiences. One summer day I was in Rhode Island near the Coast Guard station fishing for flounders. Soon one fisherman came in with a big bass in his small boat and I asked him where he caught it. He told me and I jumped into my boat, started motor and took off without telling anyone. I had some big plugs my father had made and I felt I could catch a good size fish. It was near twilight when I headed out to the fishing area. I went out a couple of miles, did some trolling with lures but did not have any success so I decided to head back to the docks. The waves were building up as I headed back. As the boat headed down one wave another one came up; crash into the boat and threw me overboard. As I came up to the surface the boat and propeller ran over me. The propeller hit me in the head but didn't knock me out as the boat continued to circle in wider and wider circles. I was dazed and my head ached as I put my hand to my head. There was a very large hole where my cheek should have been. I could just about see the shore in the distance so I started to swim towards it. About 45 minutes later I realized I was losing lots of blood. I went under several times and about the third time another boat cruising by saw my situation, motored over and grab me by my hair. This 34 foot cabin cruiser with its crew said I looked a mess. They covered me up with a blanket so as not to look at me and headed to the local Red Cross station. I severed many nerves in my cheek and 57 stitches later they released me. I spent a few days in the hospital in Stonington, Connecticut. My left eye stayed red and swollen for about one year due to the accident.

It was the evening of November 2, 1981 when I caught the 73 pound striped bass at Nauset Beach, Cape Cod. The waters were alive with bait fish that night. There were squid, sand eels and even codfish breaking water every night. We were catching cod on small plugs with teases right from the surf. It was just a phenomenal season for fishing. The weather was decent for this time of year. Remember it was early November and it was Cape Cod. The night before I had caught a 30 pound bass and a 12 pound cod. I was fishing with an eel with a big dropper in front of it. It was dead calm that eventful evening. I never saw the surf so quiet, not ever. There were just a handful of fishermen stretched out along the shoreline. The area where I fished was called "The Pouchet", located at the extreme south of Nauset Beach. It is shaped like a fishing bowl. I went to the bowl as the tide was just coming in and I could see the swirling action of big bass as they chased baitfish. The baitfish were trapped and the bass knew it but they would not hit any lures that were thrown at them. Other anglers even finished with bobbers like you would for fresh water pan fish. Nothing seems to work although we could see they were there. How could this be?

Finally I put on a big black dropper in front of the eel and that 73 pound bass hit the dropper not eel. He must have seen that eel chasing the teaser and he got there first. That was an amazing sight. You never know what bass will hit; that's what makes them such a great yet frustrating game fish. It was about a good 20 minutes battling with this big 73 pounder. One long run out of the bowl and almost to the sandbar. Then I stopped him but he made another run. He made it to the other side of the sandbar and I thought that was the end for me. Game over; you win, but …….

Gently I coaxed him back over the bar and back into the bowl. The swells of the surf that night were not against me. This was a lucky break. I patiently worked him near the beach but there was no one to help beach the fish. There was a little sliver of moonlight that evening which helped me judge next swell.

A small swell lifted the bass up just enough to put half of it on the sand while the other half was still in the water. The fish was so thick it could not help itself back into the water. I took a few quick steps, put my entire forearm in his gills and scrambled up the sand. We were catching a lots of big fish this particular year but I freaked out when I saw the size of this one. This was a season for great big bass up and down the Cape Cod coastline.

I used a Penn 750 SS spinning reel and a Lamiglas surf with 20 pound test mono line.

Steve Petrie of Long Island, New York caught his big bass a few weeks before mine at the same place. His bass probably came out of the same school. This was a massive school of big bass that moved down the coast that year. It was a memorable year. I still can recall most of the successes I had that season.

The newspapers and television interviewed me because it was a world record striped bass at that time. They came down to the beach for the picture taking session to make everything more realistic. It was weighed at two local bait and tackle shops the next day but that night I rolled it up in a woolen blanket and put it in the back of my car. That was a big mistake. The fish probably lost a few pounds being dried out all night long wrapped in the blanket. The bass unofficially weighed over 80 pounds when I weighed it at my house that evening. Too bad there goes my long lasting world record. In those days especially in the year 1981, we were getting so many big bass that I failed to realize that this one was bigger than all the others I had seen or heard about. Remember many of these bass were sold for income. Not realizing this bass could have been a world record for a long time, I thought of selling it myself. Many of the other fishermen were doing the same thing but in 1981after 9 PM in the evening this area of Cape Cod was wrapped up. The tackle shops were usually dose at sunset or there about. There was nothing open at this time. Again this was a lucky break for me. I probably would have sold it if I found a place that was open. It was also an unlucky break since I couldn't get it officially weighted.

I always had a love affair with the striped bass. My father was a great fisherman and taught me how to fish well and to have an empathy towards this species of fish. It has brought me great joy as well as opportunities to meet other successful people in their profession. I had many opportunities to interact with manufacturers whose products I had used to catch great fish. Later I did some traveling, some seminars and continual requests to be a guide for surf fishermen to these great fishing areas of Cape Cod. This soon led to my salt water guide service which I still have today.

Making a living via this fish was never attained. Many people were very happy about my success, especially Mr. Rodon who made fly rods. I did not know him at that time but he heard of this great fish and gave me everything concerning his product line to be use for my fishing activities. Saltwater fly fishing has become part of my activities especially as a guide for other fly rod fishermen. Fly rod fishing for stripers from the surf may be the ultimate fishing experience.

Jack Fallon, outdoors writer, and I became very close friends due to this fish. A lot of people in this field became friends of mine and I learned about their business as well as they learned about my skills.

Although I have not tried to obtain a trademark, I have developed many lures over the years. My dad developed an eel called Mr. Wiggley. It is a hard plug to make and when made well, it works terrifically.

Since 1982 I have been guiding men, women, teaching the young and old how to surf fish. From 6 PM to 11PM I instruct them, where and how to catch this great fish. I really enjoy this part of my business. The rest of the time is spent in the print shop where I have spent the last 20 years working with printing machines.

In the wintertime I do saltwater seminars as well as continue with my water color prints. It is my other business career.

A surf fisherman life is a "love affair" with nature and fishing for striped bass is the most exciting and most memorable of life experience. The striped bass is a special fish that has become more than a fish for me and for most fishermen. Whether from the surf with an 11foot surf rod throwing out plugs, tins or eels or with a 13 foot fly rod throwing out stream butterflies, it is the greatest experience you can have on Cape Cod.

One night back in 1980 I had a string of bass that weighed 1300 pounds. It broke the springs on my van. Those were the days when my average fish weighed 30 pounds. I could sell them for as little as $.25 a pound or $3.25 a pound. It was good income.

I have guided hundreds of fishermen over the years. I have a psychologist who I have guided to my striped bass fishing grounds on the Cape. Some of them have told me that if their patients would try this vocation, they would have no business. That's what fishing especially fish for striped bass can do to you. Your problems go away and your mind is focused on experiences that lead to more pleasurable things that heal mind and body. That's what the professionals say and who am I to dispute their findings.

If you are looking for a way to control your inner self by using simple self -edification activities, fishing for striped bass is an ultimate exercise as well as a rewarding one. Just ask any Cape Cod fisherman."

Charles Church

Striped Bass 73 pounds, Cuttyhunk, MA., August 17, 1913

World record all line classes

The time was long ago, the rod, reel and line may be from a different era, but the battle between man and fish was still the same as it is today.

This is the time before World War 1, the post Victorian age, street lights were gas lit if lighted at all, the horse was the means of transportation, blacksmiths made a living hammering iron, men wore woven straw hats and ladies beautiful feathered bonnets. Men had emerged from the middle-ages but still had a streak of chivalry about them and their ladies expected them to have knightly demeanor. An armor headpiece was replaced with a top hat and the lance by a wooden cane.

The South Bend Fishing catalog of 28 pages just came out in 1912 and was called "Quality Fishing Tackle." Clinton Wilt's "Little Wonder" lures were made and sold in the 1913 era. Shakespeare reels started in 1910 and Heddon lures were around at the same time. The Zig Zag wooden plugs were introduced by the Moon light Bait Company in 1908.

Charles couldn't use braided Dacron line that was invented in the 1930s or monofilament developed around 1939. He used the best available linen line thread.

It would be quite a while before these freshwater lures would be common usage by salt water anglers. The enlightened surf caster or boater might try these freshwater tools but bait is bait and it has caught fish in the briny over a long time. Tradition is hard to change. Charles B. Church used in 1913 the very best available bait he could find- the eel. Today's tradition still says the eel may be the best because it has been successfully used since at least 1913. Why break with tradition!

At this writing the eel may be placed on the endangered list due to overharvesting. Too much of a good harvest cannot be blamed on the salt water angler.

A little rowboat with a sail, a savvy oarsman, high surf in an angry sea and a wise old bass, made for a story that reflects the continuous battle which challenges all striped bass fisherman whether from surf or boat.

It was 73 pounds. A world record even before the IGFA existed but acknowledged by them since 1939; the year they were founded. It would last for 54 years when tied by Charles Cinto's 73 pound taken in the same area of Cuttyhunk1 Massachusetts and surpassed by Bob Rocchetta's 76 pounder taken at Montauk Point, July 17,1981. Charles Cinto's bass was not recognized by the IGFA as world record because he used wire line.

AI Me Reynold's world record, (All tackle record as titled by the IGFA), striped bass of 78lbs. 8 oz. caught off Atlantic City New Jersey, September 21, 1982 surpassed all of them.

Charles B. Church striped bass was 5 foot long with a 30 ½ inch girth and was at the end of his Abbie and Imbrie 6'6", 11 ounce bamboo rod where a J.B. Crock reel had 15 thread Hall line. You thought you had it hard?

Around the Cuttyhunk area it is unknown how many big bass were taken from the surrounding waters in the past as well as in the present. Secrets are secrets especially among fishermen. Commercial rod and reel fishermen made a living catching and selling these fish in the mid to late 1900s. Today Massachusetts still allows the sale of striped bass through licensed dealers likewise there are dedicated commercial fishermen who use nets, seines, etc. but are limited by the length of season, length of fish and quotas.

Cuttyhunk waters are strewn with rocks and are dangerous. Casting an eel from a small rowboat even with an oarsman must be made with caution. Staying just outside of the breakers assures them of survival for another day.

Cuttyhunk Island is made up of many small isles, which extend from Woods Hole and separates Buzzards Bay from Vineland Sound. Small rocky islands can produce a variety of water conditions. Rough surf with strong currents is the norm around these rocks. Good for the bass, a warning for boaters, especially small rowboats without motors. Charles used a small sail on the boat to help him get to the fishing area.

Since fiberglass or carbon fabric wrapped rods were yet to be invented, the salt water angler used the same rod materials as their fresh water brothers; bamboo. Stubby, rugged and durable they would last a lifetime if varnished judicially from time to time.

Reels were simple, single speed and a loaded with mostly twisted hemp, linen, cotton or even Japanese silk line. Reels like Julius Vam Hofe, Benjamin Stellar Thumezy with German silver frames, Clark Horrocks and Abbey and Imbrie sold for less than $10 and would hold 40 to 80 yards of line. Washing and carefully drying after each use was part of the day's activities. Inspecting the line for abrasion, cuts or rotted threads was a mandatory job and could be done as the line dried.

Casting an eel from the rowboat situated just behind the first breakers required a competent and an experienced oarsman. Reading the surf situation before putting the angler in the best position took skill and strength. Even when his 73 pound bass swallowed the eel the duo, angler and boatman, had to work together as a team in order to bring the bass to gaff.

After the hook- up maneuvering the boat among the rocks, while keeping the bass in front of them, was the oarsman's primary duty. His oarsman, Karl Kraut, was not mentioned on the certificate as the world record striped bass oarsman but you can imagine he played a significant role during the catching and landing of this fish as well as Charles Church himself.

In those early days of the 1900s wooden boats, bamboo fishing rods, simple single speed reels and cotton line, all had to be subservient to the experience and skill of the duo in the boat. The weak links may have been the terminal tackle including rod and reel but the two in the boat had to be mentally tough.

Charles was born in Cuttyhunk and often fished with his pals at the local club. He probably knew the hotspots around the islands but by "putting his time in"; he gained sufficient experience to subdue his world record striped bass.

From 1913 to the present Cuttyhunk Island still holds a special place in the hearts of striped bass fishermen looking for "big fish". Like Race Point, Cape Cod; Montauk Point, long Island; Sandy Hook, New Jersey and Cape Hatteras, North Carolina, the sound of white water waves and Nor'easter gale excite the passions of these anglers and create the ideal weather for striped bass.

Leave your surf waders home, replace your experience oarsman with a reliable motor, put your Grady White in drive and head out to do battle with the record bass as Charles B. Church did over 100 years ago. Good luck.

Charles B Church's story in his own words.

On August 17 in the company with my brother in law, I started out on my 13 foot boat to try my luck at striped bass fishing. We sailed down to the south side of Nashwena Island to some favorite pools of mine, for I have fished these pools for 28 years. Nashwena Island is one of the Elizabeth Islands. This group of islands extended from a Woods Hole to the Sow Light Boat and separates Buzzards Bay from Vineland Sound. We had a stiff breeze from the Southwest for three days and there was a heavy swell running and the water was quite thick, which was favorable for bass fishing.

Going through Cannapitsit it was quite rough, so I did not stop at the point but kept on down to the big bend, which is about midway of Nashwena Island. I took my little spirit sail and Karl took the oars as we neared at the shore. I noticed there was quite a lot of seaweed floating on the water, so I said to Karl, "We'll try the bend but it looks we can't fish here." I took my rod, which is made of bamboo, tip being 6'6", weight 11ounces, but weighs 11 ounces and was made by Abby and Imbrie of New York. Then I took a dry flour bag as I used live eels for bait at that time of year and took hold of and eel about 12 inches long and hooked the 7/0 limerick bass hook through the lips of the eel, which was very lively. Then I reeled the eel about 2 feet from the end of my rod, and was ready for a cast. Carl then backed the boat towards the shore, keeping her headed towards the surf, for the nearest shore, the rougher it is and we had to keep just outside of the breakers. For it was all rocks and each rock was covered with rockweed and every swell that rolled this rockweed washed in and the undertow wash it out again, ready for the next sea.

Getting close in as we dared to, I cast the eel into the surf within 2 feet of the beach and then reeled it towards me just fast enough so that it would not get under one of the many rocks that were there. When I got the eel close to the boat I noticed there was some long eelgrass on the hook, so I took a match out of my pocket and bent it onto the line about 2 feet above my hook so it would catch this eelgrass and in that way keep my eel as clear as possible. I then made another cast and felt a strike, so I said to Karl, "Hold on." But the fish did not take it.

Here I will explain a little so you will understand that when they striped bass sees an eel he swims by it, striking it with this tail, which stuns the eel, and it sinks, then he grabs the eel by the head and he swallows it. This is when you strike him. Now you see when I felt the strike I said, "Hold on" for Karl knows what's coming. If he had kept rowing I could not have let the eel sink or if I kept reeling him towards the boat he would not sink, so you see it is very important that your oarsman knows his job for in the surf it is very easy to get tipped over; both of you have to be wide awake all the time. Then I made another cast and very quickly had another strike but he would not bite, I said to Karl "He must be a small one perhaps there is another one with him. Let's try the 5 rock pool" (which is only about 100 feet to the east). Karl kept the bow of the boat off as the wind was still southwest and we soon got abreast of the pool. I then made a cast in front of the 2 inshore rocks and behind the 3 offshore ones. The eel had hardly struck the water when I had a strike and said, "This is something special." For I saw a whirl which I knew was made by a large bass. I waited for a few seconds before I struck him, for he was swimming round and round in a circle, my line lying loose on the water. I did not dare strike him up and down because a bass has a row of sandpaper teeth in the center of his upper jaw and if your line hits that, it will cut like a razor and you will lose your fish. Carl was wise to the situation as he pulled hard on one oar splashing all he could. That scared the fish and he started off for deep water, going by the boat on the west side, so I could strike him sideways and the line would draw down the side of his jaw, for all bass caught with live eels should have the hook down in their stomach if handled properly. I used a thumb- stall kit out of twine on my left thumb and just as soon as I strike the fish I hold the rod straight up in the air in my left hand, my thumb against the real, the butt pressing against my stomach.

The fish started off shore, so did Carl. It was the only place for us to save him. He took about 100 yards of the line on the first rush, then he started to roll but I reeled up on him so hard he came like lightning right for us and ran under the boat. But Carl was watching the line as well as I, and was turning the boat as fast as he could, so that when the fish ran under the boat and got to the other side, my line was ail clear. Then he made for the shore full speed. I yelled for him to pull hard to the westward, holding all the strain that the rod would stand and heading the fish to the south. I kept him clear of the 3 large rocks but he went around one large rock to the east of them. Carl backed water for all he was worth directly east till we got south and east of this rock, then we backed due south so I could draw the fish clear from the rock before he cut off my line.

It was awfully rough and the boat would write way up in the air on some of those swells so I could hardly keep my feet. I held the rod just as high as I could and we took- in about a half barrel of water, when the fish started for the boat, going out across the stern for the southeast and the offshore for about 150 yards, for I did not attempt to hold him very hard, as I wanted to get off -shore myself. I was getting tired and Carl was all wet as well as tired. The fish laid quiet till I reeled almost up and down on him, and we were in 7 fathoms of water, then he would run a short way but he was getting tired like ourselves.

We had no idea as to how large he was then. But when I undertook to raise him to the surface my rod bent so I was afraid it would break. Carl, I yelled, "For cat's sake don't lose him." He rode away from the fish and I had to bring him to top water that way. Probably I was 50 yards away from where I started to lift that fish alongside the boat. After getting him on top of the water, it was so rough and the tide was running so heavily to eastward against the southwest wind when that we had some job. Carl backed down towards the fish slowly, while I reeled in the line until I got within 50 feet, then he took- in his oars and got ready to gaff hook. I let the fish alongside but the tide set him so fast to the eastward with the sea and the wind blowing us northeast, that it was only after 3 attempts that I got him alongside, where Carl could get at him.

I knew it was all off when he reached for him, for he was never known to miss, but when he took the bass over the side of the boat I noticed he rolled in; as a rule Carl lifts them dear of the gunwale, so I said, "Some fish."

After we had weighed the fish we could hardly believe it ourselves but it certainly was a beauty, 73 pounds, good and strong. My reel was made by J.P. Crock of New York. It is a German silver reel, one that my grandfather had and its 100 years old, for I have used it for 28 years. My line is a Hall Line, 15 thread. I liked the hall line's better than any other for the reason that the dye does not come out and leave the line rotten, like the other lines and I had use a lot of them.

I was born on Cutyhunk and fish with all members of the Cuttyhunk Club. Last a year I caught 38 bass, this year only 17. I have used all kinds of bait but there is nothing like a live eel; only don't do what almost everybody else does, strike when you feel their bite, for the bite is his tail striking the eel.

I hope I have made it plain for your readers, so that those who have not caught a bass can you realize the sport there is in it.

Charles Church, August 17, 1913

Wilfred Fontaine

Striped bass 68 pounds, Charlestown,
Rhode Island, October 3, 1965

IGFA World Record - 20 pound line class

It was October 3, 1965 and Wilfred Fontaine was competing in the R. J. Schaefer Saltwater Fishing contest. He decided to try his luck at one of his favorite spots in Green Hill, Rhode Island by casting out to a small sandbar where bass like to hide. The weather was terrible. The wind was up. The surf was up. From time to time the fast moving clouds outlining the angry surf. The following is from his daughter's scrapbook and her memories of her father.

Joe Pimentle was with him but was fishing in a different area. He was battling the weather just as Wilfred was. They started fishing about 5 PM and about 10 PM had spent 5 hours without a strike. He was about to call it a night and go find Joe but on his next cast all of the sudden the bass grabbed the eel. Though years of experience as a member of the Scituate Saltwater Anglers "Sixty Pound Club" and the "Nifty 50 Club" told him this was a pretty good fish, maybe another 50 pound.

For 25 minutes he struggled fighting this fish. It was give and take with the big bass doing most of the taking. Pump and pull, then pull and pump. Wilfred tried to anticipate its every move in order to stay in front of it. The moon had slipped away by now and it was only the taut of the line against a rod that led him move to the fish. The bass ran straight out with its first run and he was concerned if it would stop. The line was on a Pen 700 spinning reel attached to a Lamiglas surf rod with 20 pound Ashway Magic Mono line. The line was running out too fast. It finally turned and swam with the current and he ran with it. Thank god it slowed down giving Wilfred a chance to guide the fish to the surf line. The waves were increasing in height and the wind was starting to blow even harder. Finally after about 20 minutes battling the fish, it was close enough to attempt to gaff it, but the fish still had plenty of fight left. Every time the fish was brought in close, it would sense the surf, turn and head back out into the white water. It had been a long day of fishing and Wilfred was getting tired but this bass kept up the fight.

Five times he carefully nursed the bass close to the surf line. Each time it sensed the breakers and took off again. What a great fish! Who was going to tire out first, she or Wilfred? How many chances will he get to land this fish? The line could break at any moment. The bass could spit out the eel as she twisted and turned in the surf. Wilfred needed help. Just then, as these thoughts were racing through his mind, his fishing buddy Joe came over to see if he had any luck. He asked, "Will do you need any help?" He was on time. Finally on the sixth attempt Joe was able to successfully gaff the lunker in between waves. With no idea the fish was a record and even though it was exhausting, Joe and Wilfred decided to continue fishing. The fish was placed on the sand and Wilfred went on to catch a 50 pound bass that night.

The next morning they finally decided that it was time to go to the weighing station. When the fish was weighed, they were stunned to hear the officials say it was 68 pounds. It had tied a world record. Even though Wilfred was advised that if he had brought the fish to be weighed immediately, it would have broken the world **twenty pound line** record. Wilfred was still ecstatic about his trophy catch. The bass was a 53 ½ inches long and had a girth of 32 ½ inches. He caught another 60 lbs. 9 oz. bass later on in October, near Narragansett, Rhode Island. Don't ask exactly where. It was a good year for 60 pounders.

He was so proud of the fish as well as exhausted that he even took the next day off. Wilfred met with Evening Journal staff photographer S. Carroll and had a photo taken that was published around the country. Carroll was so thrilled to see the big fish that he begged to have his photo taken with it. No problem, it was the biggest bass caught that year. Everybody had a chance to be photographed with it.

There are conflicting reports about where the fish was actually caught. Many of the printed articles that were published immediately after the fish was caught, stated that it was caught at Green Hill, Rhode Island while others including the plaque on the amount of fish, stated that it was caught at Charlestown, Rhode Island. This was because, being the competitive fisherman, he didn't want others to learn where he had really caught the fish. He didn't want to share one of his best spots hence he purposefully changed the location to Charlestown to mislead others. That's fair in love, war and fishing, especially fishing.

Wilfred had the fish professionally mounted by Jeanne Martel of South Attleboro, Massachusetts. She did a fantastic job with the display. The fish was even displayed at the Springfield Fair, Springfield, Massachusetts in the sporting booth operated by F and M Schaefer Brewing Company. In a letter from F and M Schaefer Brewing Company, the public relations director, advised us that Jack Woolner took movies of the mounted fish displayed at the fairs booth and used the footage on the TV show, "Dateline Boston" on February 1, 1966.

"Field and Stream Magazine" in March 22, 1966 awarded him a certificate and pin for this accomplishment. Penn Reels awarded him a new reel as well as a congratulatory letter. F and M Schaffer Brewing Company awarded him an honorary certificate for his catch in 1962 and 1966 as part of their Salt Water Fishing Contest. Likewise Ashway Line and Twine Manufacturing Company and Lamiglas Rods did the same.

The mounted trophy was proudly displayed on the Fontaine's the living room wall until they moved into a retirement center. The fish was donated to the Snug Harbor Marina where his fishing buddies hung out. To this day the striper is still on display at the Marina.

Wilfred lost his battle with cancer at age 75 in 1994. He continued to fish almost to the end. His wife Rita fondly recalled her life has a "fishermen's widow" and how she would watch Wilfred and his buddies take off for a day of fishing. They would be gone all day and often all night and she never knew the time they would return. She even admits that he did a little fishing on the morning of their wedding day. Just a little. She was still supportive of his hobby and proud when he brought home the big ones as well as the smaller ones but especially when he brought back himself.

Authors note: Prior to July 1, 1970, the IGFA asked for part of the line that had been used to catch fish. The specifications as to its line strength were assumed as listed in the manufacturer's catalog. After this date, all lines were tested as submitted with the application for a record and even past lines were tested to their strength and adjustments made to the records, if necessary.

Update by adding the members to the striped bass 60+++ Pound Club

Update the latest regulations for recreational fishing for striped bass.

THE STRIPPED BASS
60+++ POUND CLUB

Weight	Angler	Date	Place	Misc
81.88 lbs	Greg Myerson	8/6/2011	Long Island Sound	eei/Rattlesinker-boat
78.50 lbs	Albert R. McReynolds	9/21/1982	Atlantic City, NJ	l-surf
76.90 lbs	Peter Vican	7/18/2008	Block Island, Rl	e-boat
76.00 lbs	Robert A. Rocchetta	7/17/1981	Montauk Pt., NY	e-boat
75.40 lbs	Steven Franco	5/25/1992	New Haven, Cf	(--)
74.75 lbs	Blaine Anderson	5/25/2014	long Island Sound	scup-boat
74.00 lbs	Barry Wolfe	1/20/2011	Cape Henrv. VA	p-boat
73.00 lbs	Fred Barnes	1/23/2008	Fisherman's Island. VA	I
73.00 lbs	Charles B. Church	8/17/1913	Cuttyhunk, MA	e-boat
73.00 lbs	Charles E. Clinto	6/16/1967	Cuttyhunk, MA	e-boat
73.00 lbs	Tony Stezko	11/2/1921	Nauset, MA	l-surf
72.00 lbs	Emil Cherski	1926	San Joaquin Delta, CA	(--)
72.00 lbs	Edward J. Kirker	10/10/1969	Cuttvhunk. MA	(--)
71.00 lbs	John Baldino	7/14/1980	Norwalk, CT	e-boat
70.50 lbs	Joe Szabo	0	Block Island. Rl	e-surf
70.00 lbs	Chester A. Berry	9/5/1987	Orient Point, NY	(--)
69.50 lbs	Steven Petri Jr.	10/15/1981	Nauset. MA	e-surf
69.20 lbs	John Alberda	7/23/1983	Montauk Pt., NY	e-boat
69.00 lbs	Joe Alexander	(--)	Montauk Pt., NY	(--)
69.00 lbs	Thomas J. Russell	11/18/1982	Sandy Hook, NJ	surf
68.80 lbs	Syl Karminski	5/31/1905	Chatham Inlet, MA	(--)
68.80 lbs	John J. Solonis	8/5/1967	North Truro, MA	(--)
68.50 lbs	Ralph Gray	10/1/1958	North Truro, MA	l
68.50 lbs	Greg Myerson	7/2/1905	Block Island, Rl	e-boat
68.50 lbs	James Patterson	5/15/1905	(--)	(--)

68.08 lbs	Clay Armstrong	4/4/2006	Virginia Beach, VA	e-boat
68.00 lbs	Wilfred Fontaine	10/3/1965	Green Hill, RI	l-boat
67.60 lbs	Harold Hussey	6/8/1963	Cuttyhunk, MA	l-boat
67.50 lbs	Donald Riesgraf	6/29/1905	Virginia Beach, VA	(--)
67.50 lbs	Devlin Nolan	5/3/1985	Bloody Point, MD	l-need lefish-su rf
67.20 lbs	Harry Hussey	6/8/1962	Cuttyhunk, MA	(--)
67.00 lbs	Tim Coleman	11/18/1985	Block Island, Rl	l-need lefish-surf
67.00 lbs	Dough Dodge	9//27/1978	Georgetown, ME	(--)
67.00 lbs	Jack Ryan	5/31/1963	Block Island, RI	(--)
66.80 lbs	Ronald A. Braun	6/27/1960	Gay Head, MA	l
66.80 lbs	Michael De Barros	8/21/1968	Cuttyhunk, MA	(--)
66.75 lbs	Steven R. Thomas	11/1/1979	Brad ley Beach, NJ	rigged eel-surf
66.50 lbs	Tom Parker	6/29/1963	Nauset, MA	(--)
66.50 lbs	Donald Nee	6/14/1962	Gay Head, MA	(--)
66.50 lbs	Dennis Kelly	7/9/1982	Orient Point, NY	(--)
66.25 lbs	Frank Mularcayk	6/4/1954	Gay Head, MA	(--)
66.00 lbs	Jim Paterson	7/14/1964	Narragansett, RI	(--)
66.00 lbs	Harold Slater	10/15/1964	Weekapague, RI	(--)
65.40 lbs	Frank Hussinger	11/12/1960	Montauk Pt., NY	eel skin
65.25 lbs	Dennis Kelly	7/17/1981	Orient Point, NY	(--)
65.10 lbs	Paul G. Cook	6/20/1960	Cuttyhunk, MA	Russelure
65.10 lbs	Roger S. Tisdale	12/2007	VA Saltwater Tourn.	boat
65.00 lbs	Neil J. Corderio	9/28/1961	Race Point, MA	p
65.10 lbs	Don De Benarndino	9/6/1971	Charlestown, Rl	eel
65.00 lbs	Jarret Binz	11/1/1985	Long Beach, NY	surf
65.00 lbs	Authur S. Clark	10/23/1936	Jamestown, Rl	eel
65.00 lbs	Maurice Levesque	9/19/1960	Charlestown, Rl	e-boat
65.00 lbs	Wendell Olsen	5/9/1951	San Joaquin River, CA	(--)
65.00 lbs	James Patterson	1960s	Point Judith, Rl	eel
64.80 lbs	Louis Katine	11/4/1958	Atlantic Beach, NY	p-surf
64.80 lbs	David Webb	8/21/1960	North Truro, MA	m-boat
64.75 lbs	Tom Rinaldi	11/18/1990	Southampton, NY	surf
64.70 lbs	Billy Legkis	11/1/1978	E. long Island, NY	bucktail-surf
64.70 lbs	Allen Sosslau	5/14/1992	Chesapeake, MD	l-boat
64.50 lbs	George T. Cheshire	11/14/2007	Virginia Beach, VA	e-boat
64.50 lbs	Joseph Elian	11/1/1974	Seaside, NJ	surf
64.50 lbs	Anthony A. Sirianni	6/25/1964	Cuttyhunk, MA	(--)
64.50 lbs	Rosa Webb	8/14/1960	North Truro, MA	m-boat
64.40 lbs	Louis J. Ammen	4/21/1956	Long Island, NY	worms-boat
64.40 lbs	Walter Lare	11/8/1958	Montauk, NY	boat
64.40 lbs	W.H. Quay	6/26/1956	Orleans, MA	b
64.30 lbs	Herbert Dickerson	6/20/1964	Cuttyhunk, MA	(--)

64.25 lbs	Jason Colby	10/14/1978	Jones Beach, NY	surf
64.10 lbs	Robert Blackwell	12/1/2007	Virginia Beach, VA	e-boat
64.00 lbs	Mike Abdow	11/1/1985	Block Island, RI	surf
64.00 lbs	Asie Espenak	6/27/1971	Swea Bright, NJ	(--)
64.00 lbs	Bill Deforest	8/20/1959	North Truro, MA	p-surf
64.00 lbs	Glen Dennis	6/6/1980	Orient Point, NY	(--)
64.00 lbs	Mark Malenovsky	11/25/1992	Montauk Point, NY	bottle neck plug-surf
64.00 lbs	Steve Smith	11/1984	Block Island, RI	surf
64.00 lbs	Peter Sparuk	1960s	Cuttvhunk, MA	(--)
63.80 lbs	Bill Gavitt	1970s	Block Island, RI	eel
63.60 lbs	Morrie Upperman	8/5/1959	Island Beach, NJ	l-boat
63.50 lbs	Kay Townsend	8/14/1960	North Truro, MA	b-boat
63.50 lbs	Bill Steadam	12/21/2011	Cheaspeake Bay	boat
63.40 lbs	R.E. Couture	7/6/1954	Brenton Reef, RI	e-boat
63.40 lbs	Frank Machadd	6/24/1966	Cape Cod Canal, MA	p
63.30 lbs	Nick Smith	12/2007	Virginia Beach, VA	e-boat
63.12 lbs	Joseph Donoa	6/13/1958	Middletown, RI	b-sur
63.00 lbs	Carolyn Brown	1/3/2004	Virginia Beach, VA	l-boat
63.00 lbs	Bill Claar	12/2007	Virginia Beach, VA	e-boat
63.00 lbs	Sherwood Lincoln	11/1983	Fishers Island, NY	m
63.00 lbs	James Mitchell	1960s	Point Judith, RI	e
62.80 lbs	Wayne J. Bellinger	9/29/1970	Cape od Bay, MA	b
62.50 lbs	Greg Myerson	2010	Montauk, NY	e-boat
62.50 lbs	Frank J. Scarpo	7/9/1969	Newport, RI	(--)
62.50 lbs	Mark Sherer	7/2008	Block Island, RI	e
62.50 lbs	Stan Nabrezny	6/26/1988	Shinnecock Inlet, NY	surf
62.40 lbs	Stephen Sonnett	7/9/1959	Cuttyhunk, MA	eelskin
62.10 lbs	Wayne Rickman	2007	Virginia Beach, VA	e-boat
62.00 lbs	Nathaniel Gifford	6/10/1959	Cuttyhunk, MA	Russelure
62.00 lbs	David Hiebert	12/29/2004	Avon, NC	I-boat
62.00 lbs	Joe Sanfrantello	1970s	Montauk Point, NY	surf
62.00 lbs	Bob Smith	6/30/1957	Boston Harbor, MA	e
62.00 lbs	Anton Van Breemen	7/8/1959	Cuttyhunk, MA	eelskin
61.80 lbs	Louis J. Ammen	6/18/1956	Uoyds Neck, NY	l
61.80 lbs	Ted Nimiroski	8/3/1959	Point Judith, RI	e
61.80 lbs	Wayne Rickman	12/2007	VA Saltwater Tourn.	Boat
61.50 lbs	Jay Bechtel	12/2007	VA Saltwater Tourn.	e-boat
61.50 lbs	Leo A. Garceau	1956	Block Island, RI	e
61.50 lbs	Nicholas Lobasso	11/17/1957	Montauk, NY	bucktail
61.50 lbs	Ace lombard	7/1965	(--)	(--)
61.50 lbs	Paul R. Moulton	1964	(--)	(--)
61.50 lbs	Tom Needham	11/19/1983	Narragansett, RI	e

61.40 lbs	Herbert H. Stone	6/14/1959	Cuttyhunk, MA	Russelure
61.40 lbs	Matthew Fine	12/2007	Virginia Beach, VA	e-boat
61.00 lbs	Alfred Anuszewski	11/22/1984	Block Island, RI	redfin-surf
61.00 lbs	Robert Callander	1970s	Rhode Island	e-surf
60.16 lbs	David Wilson	12/2007	Virginia Beach, VA	e-boat
60.00 lbs	Ted Carroll	7/26/2014	(--)	e-boat
60.00 lbs	H.K. Bramhall	6/17/1958	Cuttyhunk, MA	Russelure
60.00 lbs	Vincent G.B. Casscio	6/29/1958	Provincetown, MA	rigged eel
60.00 lbs	Richard Colagiovanni	10/1954	Watch Hill, RI	(--)
60.00 lbs	George Deitz	11/12/1960	Montauk, NY	rigged eel
60.00 lbs	G.S. Hulten	9/4/1960	Truro, MA	b
60.00 lbs	Eric Lester	5/14/2014	Hudson River, NY	b
60.00 lbs	Robert Lindholm	9/4/1960	Great Bay, Dover, NH	(--)
60.00 lbs	Ted Nimiroski	8/13/1958	Narragansett, RI	eel skin
60.00 lbs	Denny O Connell	11/22/1986	Montauk Point, NY	surf
60.00 lbs	Benard O Demers	1960s	Cuttyhunk, MA	(--)
60.00 lbs	Jim Paterson	1960s	RI	(--)
60.00 lbs	A.E. Peterson	7/19/1960	Truro, MA	(--)
60.00 lbs	Polly Rosen	7/6/1956	Cuttyhunk, MA	russelure
60.00 lbs	Louis J. Smitten	10/29/1960	Sandy Hook, NJ	l
60.00 lbs	Sherman E. Whiting	6/12/1955	Montauk, NY	sea worms
60.00 lbs	Charles VanAtta	11/15/1967	Sandy Hook, NJ	spoon

Legend:　e-eel
　　　　　p-plug
　　　　　m-mackerel
　　　　　l-lure or name of lure

The Ash way Twine Company held fishing tournaments in the 1950s and 60s. Here are some of the results.

61 lbs 12 oz.	G. Newell Hurd	1965	Cuttyhunk, MA
61 lbs 8 oz.	G. Newell Hurd	unknown	unknown
60. lbs 8 Oz.	David Simons	1965	re: Nifty Fifty News
60 lbs 1 oz.	Walt Pietruska	unknown	re: Nifty Fifty News
	Bob luce		
	Clay Armstrong		
125lbs	unknown	N. Carolina	

Table B4.1

Recreational

STATE	STATE SIZE LIMITS	BAG LIMIT	OTHER	OPEN SEASON
ME	20 - 26" OR ≥ 40"	1 fish	Hook & line only; No gaffing	All year, except spawning areas are closed 12.1 -4.30 and catch and release only 5.1 - 6.30. Spawning area includes Kennebec watershed.
NH	1 fish 28--40" & 1 fish >28" 2	2 fish	No netting or gaffing; must be landed with head and tail intact; no culling. No sale.	All year
MA	28" min	2 fish	Hook & line only	All year
RI	28" min	2 fish		All year
CT	28" min, except Connecticut River Bonus Pmgram: 22-28"	2 fish, except CR Bonus: 1 fish	CR Bonus Quota: 4,025 fish	All year, except CR Bonus 5.4-6.30 (limited to I-95 bridge to MA border)
NY	Ocean Private: 1 fish 28-40" & 1 fish > 40" Ocean Charter: 28" min Hudson River: 18" min DE River: 28" min	Ocean: 2 fish Hudson R.: 1 fish DE River: 2 fish	Angling or spearing only	Ocean: 4.15- 12.15 Hudson River: 3.16 11.30 Delaware River: All year
NJ	28" min	2 fish, plus 1 additional through Bonus Program	Bonus progtam quota: 321,750 lb. No netting. Non-offset circle hooks tequired 4.1-5.31 in DE River if using natural bait.	Atlantic Ocean no closed season. DE River & tribs open 3.1-3.31 & 6.1-12.31. All other marine waters open 3.1-12.31
PA	Non-tidal DE River: 28" min; Delaware Estuary: 28" min. except 20-26" from 4.1-5.31	2 fish		Year round
DE	28" min. except 20-26" from 7.1-8.31 in Del. River, Bay & tl'ibutaries	2 fish	Hook & line, spear (for divers) only. CircJe hooks required in spawning season.	All year except 4.1-5.31 in spawning grounds (catch release & allowed)

MD	Susquehanna Flats (SF): 18-26" Chesapeake Bay Trophy: 28" min Chesapeake Bay Regular: 18" min with 1 fish > 28" Ocean: 28" min	SF: 1 fish Chesapeake Bay Trophy: 1 fish Chesapeake Bay Regular: 2 fish Ocean: 2 fish	SF: non-off set circle hook if baited hooks & gap>0.5" Chesapeake Bay Quota: 2,956,463 lbs (part of Baywide quota; includes Susquehanna Flats harvest, excludes trophy harvest)	SF: 3.1-5.31; catch & t•elease only 3.1-5.3 Chesapeake Bay Trophy: 4.18-5.15 (most tribs closed) Chesapeake Bay Regular: 5.16-12.15 (most tribs closed until 6.1) Ocean: All year
PRFC	Trophy: 28" Regular: 18" min with 1 fish > 28"	Trophy: 1 fish Regular: 2 fish	Quota: 683,967 lbs. (part of Baywide quota; excludes trophy harvest)	Trophy: 4.18 -5.15 Regular: 5.16-12.31
DC	18" min with 1 fish > 28"	2 fish	Hook & line only	5.16-12.31
VA	Quota: 683,967 lbs. (part of Baywide quota; excludes trophy harvest) Bay/Coastal Trophy: 32" min (28" Potomac tribs) CB Spring: 18-28"; 1 fish >32" CB Fall: 18-28"; 1 fish >34" Potomac Tribs: 18-28"; 1 fish >28" Ocean: 28"	Bay/Coastal Trophy: 1 fish CB Spring: 2 fish CB Fall: 2 fish Potomac Tribs: 2 fish Ocean: 2 fish	Hook & line, rod & reel, hand line only Chesapeake Bay Quota: 1,538,022lbs in 2010 (part of Baywide quota; excludes trophy harvest)	Bay Trophy: 5.1-6.15 (open 4.18 Potomac tribs) Coastal Trophy: 5.1-5.15 CB Spring: 5.16-6.15 (no fish >32" in spawning areas) CB Fall: 10.4-12.31 Potomac Tribs: 5.16-12.31 Ocean: 1.1-3.31, 5.16-12.31
NC	Roanoke River: 2 fish 18-22" OR 1 fish 18-22" and 1 fish > 27" Albemarle Sound: 18" min. Ocean: 28" min	Roanoke River: 2 fish Albemarle Sound: 3 fish Ocean: 2 fish	Roanoke River quota: 137,500 lb. Albemarle Sound quota: 137,500 lb.	Roanoke River: 3.1 -4.30 (single barb less hook required 3.1-6.30 from Roanoke Rapids dam downstream to US 258 bridge) Albemarle Sound: Spring 1.1 4.30; Fall 10.1-12.31 Ocean: All year

INDEX